D0944950

THE CHIME CHILD

ML
3652
.T65

THE CHIME CHILD

or

Somerset Singers

*Being an account of some of them
and their songs collected over
sixty years*

by

RUTH L. TONGUE

FOLKLORE ASSOCIATES
HATBORO, PENNSYLVANIA

LONDON
ROUTLEDGE & KEGAN PAUL

WITHDRAWN

183388

First published 1967
by Routledge & Kegan Paul Ltd
Broadway House, 68–74 Carter Lane
London E.C.4

Printed in Great Britain
by W & J Mackay & Co Ltd
Chatham, Kent

© *Ruth L. Tongue 1967*

No part of this book may be reproduced
in any form without permission from
the publisher, except for the quotation
of brief passages in criticism

SBN 7100 2967 5

Owing to production
delays this book was
published in 1968

Dedicated to Richard Garland
the Sedgemoor Soldier
killed in France 1917

Foreword

It was the 'Carol of the Beasts' from Nailsbourne, sent in manuscript by Ruth Tongue as a Christmas card, that first introduced me to the tremendous store of folk material she had collected over many years. At that time she had hardly begun to prepare it for publication, but she allowed me to make trio arrangements of some of the songs for a small Cotswold choir. 'Enchanting,' said one sophisticated listener, 'but surely not genuine folk song? It's too good to be true'. Most collectors must have encountered similar remarks, because folk music and poetry do indeed range from the ridiculous to the sublime, and the best examples are of astonishingly high quality.

Ruth Tongue has been collecting almost since infancy. Being a Minister's daughter was no disadvantage: the people of West Somerset accepted her as a 'gifted' child who would speak their language and share their secrets. She kept the treasures to herself for half a century, and only when it was clear that they were in danger of disappearing for ever did she decide to put them on permanent record. The manuscript of *The Chime Child*, with its vivid procession of West-country characters, came first to the *Countryman* office and we published two composite extracts from it in Autumn and Winter, 1965. Otherwise none of the material has appeared before, nor have any of the song tunes been in printed collections, except 'I took my Dame to Lambing Feast' which is sung to the well-known air of 'Abram Brown' or 'The Quaker's Wife'.

Most folk songs have more than one setting, just as many folk tunes are used for several different sets of words. Folk singers often vary time and tune as they go along, which helps to give

folk music its remarkable variety. Asked to check the notation of
The Chime Child songs, I did so only after listening long and carefully to a tape-recording made by Ruth Tongue and a Somerset
friend of hers. As space did not permit the inclusion of all possible
versions, we decided to use only those that have not been published before. Variations in tempo have been indicated as a rule by
a pause mark rather than by inserting an extra beat in the bar, for
these long-drawn-out notes are characteristic of most folk singers
and are not integral to the tunes.

Here then are Old Shepherd, Gillavor of Taunton Barracks,
Annie's Granny, Richard Garland the Sedgemoor soldier, Cordelia
Cooper the gipsy, Mr. Barry the ballad singer, wicked Isaiah Sully
and the rest, to speak and sing for themselves as they did to the
eagerly listening Chime Child long ago.

FAITH SHARP

The Countryman
Burford, Oxford
14th December 1966

Contents

Foreword by Faith Sharp   *page* vii

Author's Note   x

1   The Chime Children   1

2   'Old Shepherd'   5

3   A Taunton Trio   13

4   'Gillavor'   18

5   William Webber   23

6   Two Aunties and a Great-Great-Granny   28

7   Annie's Granny   35

8   Richard Garland, the Sedgemoor Soldier   45

9   Delilah Odcombe   50

10 Seafarers from the Severn Sea   56

11 Mrs. Cordelia Cooper   62

12 Mr. Barry, the Ballad Singer   68

13 Isaiah Sully   74

    The Music of the Songs   85

    Index of Names and Song Titles   101

Author's Note

I am not a musician, nor an expert, nor an academic student in the matter of these old songs. I sang them myself for my own enjoyment and therefore they comprise a cross-section of rescued melodies dating back to medieval days and up to the Victorian early ballads. Very few can be less than a hundred years old, many of my fellow singers reaching back to a youth spent in George IV's reign, and I do not think they have been collected before. To those who love old songs and their singers I hope they will give as much pleasure as I found in sixty years and more of listening to, and singing, their songs and sharing their company.

Among many country people there still lingers the age-old dislike of being mentioned by name. 'I'll sing for 'ee gladly but yew mustn't put my name to it.' I have, therefore, out of respect for this feeling and those of friends and relatives, substituted other names for those of the singers described.

I

The Chime Children

In this modern age of televised 'occult' discussions for the millions on matters our forefathers wisely regarded as 'best not talked about', I have often been asked by fellow folklorists to explain a Chime Child.

I have, at last, felt free to do so. For years the ancient command of silence and secrecy held me back, although I had quite deliberately and prayerfully done what I could to remove that foot of mine so firmly planted in an unseen world. There are many men and women in this too-glib world of interviews and trivial chatter, who are still known to be 'Seers', 'Seventh Children of Seventh Children', 'the gifted', the charmer (*not* the fortune teller), who have been born to a strange heritage, and live out their lives with a foot in each of the worlds, seen and unseen. They are usually very silent about it, and only very few friends or their families know. Most of these 'traditional namings' are to be found, through our modern passion for scientific classification, in various dictionaries but I doubt if you will find more than one reference to a Chime Child. The Chime Hours, yes—those potent ghostly hours from midnight to cock-crow that Shakespeare and his forbears knew were dangerous to living man because the Powers of Darkness claimed them—these you will find in many records of many beliefs. But a Chime Child was a purely local West Somerset faith, and within my own lifetime faded, with so much ancient lore that did not survive the First World War. So here is a description of what the very old in the 1900's declared Chime Children to be.

They must be born between midnight on a Friday and cock-crow on a Saturday, as I am told I was—both these days being regarded as full of unseen danger among some villagers. This was all explained to me before I was five.

1

I had been out for a walk with an adult to visit our sexton's home. There was a funeral and its arrangements to be discussed. Young Sexton's wife, however, considered such talks unfit for my tender years. (Little did she know!) 'Jack and his dad be over church now, ma'am. Leave the little maid bide with Jack's mother and his old aunties. They'll like to see her.'

They did, and I was equally pleased to meet them, although by the end of our meeting there was so much in my small mind that I could only feel the warm glow of a huge secret.

In the midst of my chatter the Old Sexton's wife took my hand and drew me to her gently, asking, 'And when was you borned, my little dear?' After many questions we finally arrived at the right answer—I had been born after midnight had struck on a Friday. The old lady sat back in triumph and both the elderly aunts beamed—apparently I had done something very clever, though nobody at home had ever mentioned it. Then the right-hand Aunt—the one with two corkscrew curls—began to recite a verse. I loved words and listened eagerly.

> They that be born of a Friday's chime
> Be masters of musick and finders of rhyme,
> And every beast will do what they say,
> And every herb that do grow in the clay,
> They do see what they see and they hear what they hear,
> But they never do tell in a hundred year.

Then they all three nodded and so I nodded back. We all said the last line again, and I was an accepted Chime Child, for their ghoulish interrupted gossip now continued something like this:

SECOND AUNT (THE ONE WITH VELVET TRIMMINGS): 'So old Mrs. Buzzacot have a-goed off at last, the wicked old toad!'

FIRST AUNT (WITH THE CURLS), REGRETFULLY: 'Vicar did say she made a good end—but I *doubt* it! She'll *come again*'.[1]

SEXTON'S WIFE, FIRMLY: 'No, she won't then! Dad and young Jack they took good care of that. They turned her face down in her coffin afore they nailed it up. I don't doubt she knows which way she'm bound for and not all deceiving of Vicar, and saying she were repented will alter it'.

A general sigh of satisfaction all round and then a final triumphant statement: 'What's more, they've been and a-buried her on top of the Dog!'

ME (VERY SORRY FOR HIM AND WONDERING IF MRS BUZZACOT HAD BEEN VERY FAT): 'What dog?'

FIRST AUNT: 'Why, the Church Dog to be sure as is always buried somewhere on the North side to drive Old Nicky away, but there, you'm a Chime Child and know about all they things!'

And strangely enough I discovered I did, and a lovely, terrible, wonderful world it was that I had one foot inside—making very sure of the sanctuary in which the other every-day foot remained rooted. And in my childhood and for fifty long years after 'I never did tell'.

And these are the gifts of Chime Children even if they never realize they have them:

1 To see the dead and the fairies, and speak with them but come to no harm—such encounters must never be sought.

2 To have immunity from all ill-wishing, as many of the clergy have.

3 To love and control all animals—so Chime Children often become herdsmen or veterinary surgeons.

4 To have a knowledge of herbs and a way of healing others.

---

[1] *Come again*—haunt.

3

A strange heritage which in old times would have meant accusations of witchcraft, but nowadays has helped to staff surgeries and hospitals. Like myself others have tried to come to terms with their 'gifts' for the benefit of other folk—while those whose curiosity or vanity tempted them to venture further into a world unseen have, as the tales of thousands of years give warning, perished miserably and spiritually.

It is never wise for man to know too much, his understanding is still very limited and minute, so like the country people who have always been very close to old Mother Earth and her ways—'best let bide'.

2

'Old Shepherd'

Folk-singer and musician,
born about 1815, died about 1903

He was the very first singer I knew and I have loved him all my life. We met when he was very old and I was very tiny, but it was enduring love at first sight. I saw him only twice but my heart warms at the very thought of him even now. For it was he who first opened the magic doors of folk music to me, and his songs and tunes still crop up to bring keen pleasure in my years of collecting.

Our first meeting was outside a small country church. It was a time of Harvest Thanksgiving, and, half pagan as the area was in many matters, they had decorated the foot of the pulpit with a large sheaf of corn which they called 'the dolly', and to bring luck to the service and the coming year it must be wreathed or stuck with flowers by the youngest maiden; ''twas the custom'. Although a visitor I was the youngest maiden capable of toddling into the church handfast with a proud farm-girl. Once face to face with the rustling giant towering above me, I was given a bunch of marigolds ('must be the right flowers, mind') and told to get on with the decorating. I sat myself down on the cold stone floor and went to it with alacrity. Alas! marigolds are not the easiest of flowers for very little fingers, and after I had decapitated about five of them my disappointment and the coldness of my small behind amalgamated into heart-broken disapproval. The lynx-eyed girl watching my face begin to pucker tucked me under one arm, and had whisked me out through the church porch before my tears

5

should outrage the sanctity and break the luck—and then the lusty bellowing began and she was kept captive in the churchyard, missing all the excitement.

An old man came up the path with a carefully combed and washed hank of sheep's wool. He put it down gently among the other porch-offerings and as gently took me from her willing clasp and carried me down the path away from the church

Even in my sorrows I was interested in him because he was wearing a night-shirt in day time. I had never seen the old linen round frock and I was to see very few more. They had gone out of fashion years since but Old Shepherd always wore his—'They'll see me out', he said, and they did.

Now he carried me, still squalling, and sat down in the sunshine on the grass-banked church wall, took me on his knee and began to sing, as if I were one of the great-grandchildren for whom he had composed the song, and from whom in later years I learned the whole of it. I stopped abruptly in the middle of a howl, my mouth now open in amazement, one fat tear still acreep down my face.

And this is what he sang:

[TUNE ONE]

THE BOLD PIGLET

Composed and sung by 'Old Shepherd', Blackdown Hills, 1901.

There were a liddle piglet, he wadn't very old,
He runned away from whoame he did, he were so very bold.

He went into the Orchet, the apples he did eat,
Says Varmer to his Missus—' 'Twill make the bacon sweet.'

He went into the Tallat[1] and chuffled with his snout,
And everyone was sneezing—the meal was all about.

He went into the Hen house to try and steal some eggs,
The hens set up a cackling and pecked his little legs.

He went into the Stable, the oats was laying thick,
The ponies all did lift a foot and so he run out quick.

He went into the Barton,[2] the cows was all a-row,
He squeal and say, 'I'm thirsty'—and they say, 'Whoame
you go!'

He went whoame to his mother and whatever do 'ee think?
The others been before him and left him nought to drink.

Now all yew liddle children that has your bite and sup,
Before you takes to travelling *just eat it all right up!*

I sat enchanted while a horny finger gently mopped up the
tears, and I looked up into an old weather-beaten, wrinkled face
with faded blue eyes and thought he was God or Father Christmas.
Words I had met up with through the royal road of 'This choogey
pig went to market' and 'There were two blackbirds sitting on a
hill'. I had even graduated to 'A little Cock Sparrow sat on a tree'.
Music I had discovered against a terrifying expanse of sea and sky
and a comforting voice that sang far below. We were at Clovelly,
and the owner of the voice was a fisherman singing, 'Heave away,
my Johnny' but the words at that distance below were lost. Now
here were both words and music—a wonderful thought.

[1] Tallat—a meal-loft reached by an outside stair.
[2] Barton—cowshed.

The next and last time we were to meet was when he came into the farm kitchen for something he needed. I recognized the night-shirt and clasping one neatly yorked leg clamoured, 'Pig! Pig, please.' Once again I was lifted up close to that dear old face and this time he sang another two verses about a sheep dog.

Here were more words and more music, and then and there I determined to go seeking this enchantment wherever I went— and I'm still doing it. Old Shepherd had done the same all his long life, thinking them out to fill the long empty days alone with his herd except for his collie; and many of them have a feeling of open air shining through them. 'The Shepherd and his dog' was a great favourite of his and his large family.

[TUNE TWO]

THE SHEPHERD AND HIS DOG

Composed and sung by 'Old Shepherd', Blackdown Hills, 1870–1903.

> They be climbing up the hill,
> All our sheep, all our sheep,
> For the morning air be chill,
> And the fields they lie still,
> And the wordle[1] be asleep,
> Say the Shepherd and his dog.

> Now the sun be all aglow,
> All our sheep, all our sheep,
> They do take their way below,
> Where the little streams do go,
> And the sweetest of keep,
> Say the Shepherd and his dog.

[1] Wordle—world.

8

Now we bring them whoame to fold,
All our sheep, all our sheep,
For the moon be rising gold,
And the evening air blows cold,
Down over the steep,
Say the Shepherd and his dog.

Oh the lambs be coming too,
All our sheep, all our sheep,
Trittle-trotting by each ewe,
Every fleece adrench with dew,
All our pretty, pretty sheep,
Say the Shepherd and his dog.

He had been a shepherd all his life along his Devon Somerset
borderland and even now his songs crop up in Blackdown homes,
or dances that have his tunes are used by local dance-bands. I never
heard that he played any instrument, but I expect, like most
country lads, he had made elder pipes and enjoyed those. Some
of his tunes have that quality. He lived a remote, placid life
and never made any stir with his gift for clear rhythm and
rhyme.

It is only now that I am beginning to make a quite remarkable
collection—most people telling me ' 'Tis one of the Old Shepherd's', but who he was they have no idea.

He rightly belonged to a much earlier age than ours; I doubt if
he ever saw a train, and a motor-car was still being frowned upon
by all horse owners in the year he died. All one can gather now
is that he was greatly loved and admired in his time.

But I love him still and give daily thanks that we sat on that
churchyard wall together.

'OLD SHEPHERD'

[TUNE THREE]

TENDING THE SHEEP

Composed and sung by 'Old Shepherd', Blackdown Hills, 1870–1900.

If I were the King of Tan'ton Town,[1]
I'd wear a sword and a golden crown,
I'd ride on afore when we went to the war,
With soldiers to follow, a hundred or more!

But   *I'd rather be tending my sheep—Yes, I'd rather be*
        tending my sheep,
        My ewes and my rams and my little young lambs,
        I'd rather be tending my sheep.

If I were a Bristol merchant-man,
With silver to collar and silver to hem,
And fine chests of gold a sight to behold,
The thieves and the robbers would soon make me old.

So   *I'd rather be watching my sheep, etc.*

A shepherd I been all the days I have seen,
When the fields they are white, when the leaves they
    are green,
I do meet with my foe when the cold wind do blow
And they voxes so cunning hide down in the snow.

But   *I'd sooner be guarding my sheep, etc.*

[1] Tan'ton—Taunton.

10

'OLD SHEPHERD'

[TUNE FOUR]

BABEL TOWER

Composed by 'Old Shepherd', Blackdown Hills, 1828.

When man first began he 'ood listen to advice,
He were loving to his mother,
He were kind to his brother,
And God said,
'That's very nice.'

But when he built a Tower he did quarrel and fight,
And he did stamp and shout,
And he laid his fists about,
And God said,
'That's not right.'

Then they all cried out together and the noise went
near and far,
But no-one understood,
And they couldn't if they would,
And God said,
'There you are!'

NOTE The Almighty was evidently from Blackdown since His pronouncements are pure Somerset vernacular:

> That's very nice
> That's not right
> There you are!

An acquaintance of mine did post-War social work among Old People's

Homes and Clubs in South London, and sent me this: 'I've got something written down for your collection. I got nurse to do it while everyone was listening and singing it. It was very popular with them, and so was the Somerset old lady who was persuaded to perform for me. She didn't need much persuading for they all knew about it and promised to join in—"Yew see, miss, we used to sing it down Chapel when I were young (1880's). There was a very clever shepherd out our way, and he made it up. He'd a bewtiful voice to sing, and he made up songs for them to dance to as well. It come about this way, he'd a whole parcel of brothers and sisters not a bit like him—he were always peaceable, and they were forever down-arging[1] and pummelling till his poor mother were at her wits end. 'I'll stop 'en, Mother,' he say, and he was but a lad thirteen. And he sang out and they all listen. There wasn't no more clack-magging[2] in that whoame." '

[1] Down-arging—wrangling.
[2] Clack-magging—hubbub.

3

A Taunton Trio

Alice Hagarty and Delia and Patrick Flynn,
laundresses and navvy
Taunton Castle, Christmas-tide 1906

I was sitting somewhat disconsolately upon the wide window-seat
of our nursery in Castle House gazing out upon a greying Cattle
Market Place with no beasts in it, for it was only two days to
Christmas. There were no horses being trotted up and down just below, there was only wet wintry dusk and the long deadly gap of time
till Christmas really dawned; and then I heard faint distant singing.

Right inside *our* house!—the Minister's house!

Of course, he was out on his pastoral visits for the week, and
mother was down at a Church Sewing Meeting and my eldest
brother was cross-country running near Milverton in a cheerful
welter of Tone waters, farmyard mire, abrasions and perspiration,
and we two children were supposed to be safely tucked away far
up in an attic nursery. So what had happened to Kate, the guardian
sentry in the great kitchen far below?

I looked hopefully at my younger brother, deep in our dilapidated armchair drawn right up to the nursery fire, doubly deep
in the war-whoops and tomahawks of 'The Scalp Hunters'; and
decided to rescue Kate alone.

At the top of the twisting stair I hesitated in the winter dusk
with the thought of the scary downward journey, but the singing
was now loud and very cheerful. If our pale quiet Kate had not
been killed she was enjoying herself, and I could do with a little
enjoyment of my own.

13

The singing, wordless but cheerful, now swelled into a clatter of boots.

I went down, without any thought of the Monmouth Ghost I had seen in August, along the bedroom passage, and crossed the huge expanse of paved hall floor to the nail-studded medieval door of the kitchen.

The cheerful singing and chatter had stopped abruptly and a soft crooning had taken its place. It was lovely and I wanted to get close to it, besides I still didn't know what had happened to Kate. I slowly pushed back the huge door and slid into the stone-paved kitchen.

'There!' said Kate's voice very cheerfully. 'I told 'ee to sing quiet—you've a-brought Miss Ruthie all downstairs in the dark before the tea-bell. Against her mother's wishes too—but there, that child will venture anywhere for a song!'

Something had happened to Kate indeed—she was for once a Christmas-tide hostess in an old empty castle, the Christmas Spirit engulfed her, and our kitchen became a place of revelry. Very mild revelry it was, but astonishing in our nonconformist home, for Kate had two visitors to keep her company in that off-time between washing-up and tea-trays, and they were both laundresses, both Irish, and strangest of all they were both Catholics.

Most of Edwardian Taunton shuddered at such a source of plagues in the midst of our town that had suffered martyrdom for King Monmouth, and the braver of father's congregation would have hastened to pluck me away.

But no, perhaps not now. Two zealous ladies had taken me aside the previous week while walking home with a small Catholic school-friend. They had whispered in ghoulish horror, 'Ruthie dear, that little girl is a *Catholic*. Does your dear father know?'

My answer was prompt and clear. I was known to be a devastating child. 'He wouldn't mind if he did—He talks with Father Brannigan!'

14

Such earthquake shocks of horror to narrow puritan spinsterhood were met courageously by sickly smiles and the approving comment, 'How nice of you to know her, Ruthie dear.'

And my instant retort, 'How nice of her to know me,' delivered as clearly and cheerfully as before, terminated what must have been a painful scene for many of the watching faithful.

And as for Kate's visitors, one of them was Alice, Kate's lifelong, Somerset born and bred, Irish friend, and mother knew all about Alice, saying so quietly and firmly to the would-be-shocked of the Mothers' Meeting. Both my parents had a wide Christianity and so I supposed that Delia had been included too—as she would be as soon as mother met her.

Mrs. Delia Flynn was shaped like a cottage-loaf under the patched top-coat that her Patrick was not wearing for a few hours so that she could go visiting in it; and, from her battered patched men's boots to her scrawny dragged-back knob of hair pulled tight from a face as round and red as a polished apple, I considered her altogether beautiful. She chuckled often like a blackbird and, though I could understand Alice's and Patrick's acquired westcountry burr with a flavour of some other accent that made their speaking exciting, with Delia it was all excitement, even if I lost myself in the music of a strange brogue.

The echo of the clatter of boots had long passed, and if there had been a decorous jigging it, too, was lost to me—I clutched desperately at fast departing magic, 'What was that carol? I heard it—outside the door.'

There was a rather worried silence.

There *was* a carol—but it was a Catholic carol (as two-thirds of our oldest and loveliest are) but worse still, it was one of Patrick's own, the fine man with the words that he was, and Father Brannigan had let it be sung by the three of them in the Chapel itself, but to sing it under the roof of Kate's own noncomformist minister could not be thought of.

15

So after the opening vistas of Heaven followed desolation.

I didn't cry, I rarely did, but just turned in blind obedient despair to face the black road upstairs to the lamplit nursery in company with the Monmouth Ghost.

Delia could not bear it. She flung a fat scrubbed arm round me. 'Ah, the poor little scrap, and why wouldn't she be singing about Donkeys, and her the bold gerrul that she is!'

'Donkeys!' said the bold girl, dazed by yet another whisking to unknown heights of delight.

'Will you be listening then and singing?' demanded Delia.

It seemed an order impossible of execution, but in that magic hour I managed both. We all did, even Kate who never whispered above one note, and mother came back and opened the door on our final Alleluias.

[TUNE FIVE]

THE CAROL OF CHRIST'S DONKEY

Sung and words composed or filled in from older fragments by Patrick Flynn, born in Somerset 1876. Sung with him at Taunton, Christmas 1906 by his twin sister, Alice Hagarty, born 1876, and by his wife, Delia Flynn of Dublin, born 1880.

> I gave Him my manger all full of sweet hay;
> I knelt with the shepherds on Chrissimas Day.
> The Star it shone over and loud did I bray.
> Gloria in excelsis! Christ the Lord is born!
>
> I carried Him softly on Egypt's dark road;
> King Herod was angered to find we had goed.[1]

[1] *Goed*—gone. This is pure grammatical Somerset from Saxon times.

16

His soldiers had stayed us afore, had he knowed.
Jubilate! Amen! Christ the Lord is free!

I carried Him proudly on Palm Sun-en-day;
On leaves of the Tree I did walk all the way.
The people rejoiced, they did carol and say,
Hosanna in the Highest! Christ the Lord is King.

They lifted Him down from the cruel Cross-tree;
And sadly I bore Him to Gethsemane.
My tears fell so fast that I hardly could see.
Miserere Domine! Christ the Lord is dead and gone.

Our Lord He is risen! He walks by the sea.
A Cross on my back for the world for to see.
Now blest be all Donkeys! Now blessèd be He!
Alleluia! Alleluia! Christ the Lord is King of Heaven.

The carol ended, the visitors with polite thanks separated and
before mother could spoil her own pleasure by dutiful enquiry as
to my presence out of the nursery, Kate tactfully rang the tea-bell.

My brothers, one still wrapped in an aura of scalping parties
daunting to seventeenth-century ghosts, the other reeking of mud,
blood and general farmyard boot-carried muck, both descended on
us demanding bread and butter and soap and towels. The front
door was opened and the Minister came home to a well-ordered
Puritan household.

NOTE The donkey superstitions so lovingly embodied in this carol
include its power of speech on Christmas Eve, its shedding of tears, and
the proof of its holiness—its black cross.

17

4

'Gillavor'

Taunton Courts, behind St. Mary's, 1906

In my childhood Taunton abounded in late medieval courts, almshouses and overhanging ancient shops, all swept away now to provide arid empty spaces for the parking of man's mechanical tyrant, the motor-car. The old picturesque lines of irregular roofs, tiny paved yards and flower plots a yard and a half square somehow bright with flower slips from village gardens were a joy to the eye if not to the nose. Some of the courts behind St Mary's were insanitary slums, crowded with children of every age and in every ragged garment conceivable, among them the fever-ridden and such of the deformed as our modern children would run from in unbelieving horror. The chance of meeting one of the distorted and hunch-backed even in the Parade cast a shadow over my every venture along the Taunton streets, and I developed a swift talent for dodging into doorways to avoid sights of malformed or mal-treated mankind which haunted my dreams for long years.

That I should venture into such strongholds of nightmare was, of course, unbelievable, and yet when I heard, above the racket of crying babies and quarrelling adults, a stream of melody on a violin, I followed till I found it.

Not all the courts were dens of filth nor all the tenants evil; there were also the clean-living but very poor, such as Delia and her Patrick who worked twenty-four hours a day to rent a whole cottage for their young brood.

The rent was 1s. 6d. and the cottage minute and full of the steam of Delia's washing-tub, but the Flynns were considered the aristocracy of their immediate circle. Their court, kept spotless with the constant suds of Delia's laundering, had a pump of its own, and in summer the yard was crossed with lines of drying sheets and linen, while youthful Flynns who had reached years of usefulness were to be seen in all directions carrying snowy bundles of washing to the select backdoors of Mount Street and even of Haines Hill.

Next door to the Flynn's cottage lived an army pensioner with only one leg, who kept his flower knot a delight to the eye and a pleasure to the nose after the other courts. He even grew roses up his cottage with the aid of the soap suds. The third cottage held a pair of retired servants, meticulously neat and tidy and prim-mannered, finding in their bare existence much Christian comfort in the Bible openly displayed in their downstairs window and the wise cat who shared the window with the Bible and never ventured beyond the bastion of the Flynn's cottage, keeping itself fatter than its owners by reducing the rodent population daily.

The next cottage to the respectable couple belonged for a brief while to 'Gillavor'. She had the looks to earn a dozen rents, and she had Taunton barracks to augment such earnings, but her cottage had a doorstep as clean as the soap suds could make it, there was a cracked bow-pot of country flowers in her window, and none of her suitors ever entered the court, hanging round in less savoury doorways till she emerged on her sinful way.

It was, then, to this court that the soldier's violin drew me through the turmoil and terror that still have power to haunt me. Delia was horrified, but promised Patrick's protection back to safer streets, and meanwhile since the little 'gerrul' wanted music, the court supplied it. Such of the regiment of Flynns as were not afield carrying washing back, sang; Patrick, off work and at home with a damaged foot but capable of turning the mangle, sang and turned, and Delia sang and washed; the pensioner played dances on a squeaky violin, and the neat old couple sat side by side on their doorstep and added a methody hymn. It was delightful and

19

exciting but it wasn't quite what I was seeking. Then in the doorway of the last cottage a thin listless woman appeared with too
bright eyes and vivid red cheeks, and she sang too. The court
listened in a silence that was courteous and full of real Christian
pity, and I listened in rapture. She would have been a well-built
country lass with clear eyes and healthy laughter if the old dreary
tale of disillusion had not driven her steps to the courts and the
barracks. She would only be 'following the drum' a very brief
while longer for she had a bad cough and the soap suds must have
made it worse, but her natural liking was for the clean and simple
and so she sang me 'Gillavor White and Rosy Red' and 'The Posy
Rhyme' before she coughed again and went in and shut her door.

[TUNE SIX]
GILLAVOR WHITE AND ROSY RED

*Sung in the courts behind St. Mary Magdalen by a young woman, Taunton
1906.*

Gillavor, Gillavor, white and rosy red,
Tell me truly if I shall wed.
Shall I be a widow, a mother or a wife,
Or shall I live single all my life?
Tell me,
What shall it be,
A widow, wife or single all my life?
For he loves me, he don't,
He'll have me, he won't,
He would if he could but he can't.

Gillavor, Gillavor, white and rosy red,
Tell me truly who shall I wed?
Tinker, tailor, soldier, sailor out at sea,
20

Or a soldier, a soldier, far from me?
Tell me,
Who shall it be,
A tailor, a soldier, far from me?

Gillavor, Gillavor, white and rosy red,
Tell me truly when I shall wed,
This year, or next year or sometime 'twill be
Or shall it be never—never for me?
Tell me,
When shall it be?
This year, or next year, or *never* for me?

Patrick hobbled with me to St. Mary's, and said gravely, 'Now, I'm telling you 'tisn't the place for you, Miss Ruthie. I shall have to be seeing your Dad if you come again.'

I was rather hurt by this, though relieved at the silence as to my invasion; but I was determined to see Gillavor again and get more of her country songs. I chose a day when Patrick was back at his navvying and Delia was invisible in a cloud of steam, but this time it was the elderly couple who saw me safely away. There was no singing—there was no Gillavor. The end cottage was empty since that morning's pauper-funeral, and the bow-pot was gone from the window.

NOTE There are two other verses taken from the Cherry-Stones Game 'Where shall I live?' and 'What shall I wear?'—but I think they are a local adaptation. We kept very strictly to verses 1, 2 and 3 for flower petals and rye grass as means of divination. Housing and clothing belonged to cherry-stones' counting, and transport—'Coach, carriage, dung putt, wheelbarrow'—to plums. Various villages in Taunton Deane had differing versions. This tune is one of the 'Willy Waly Wallflowers' group, a very ancient game recalling the maiden tribute of early days.

'GILLAVOR'

[TUNE SEVEN]

THE POSY RHYME

*Sung in the Courts behind St. Mary Magdalen by a young woman,
Taunton 1906.*

The daisy, the daisy, she sits in the grass,
Where little birds nest and the little lambs pass,
She grows—oh she grows—in a fine silver ring,
And when there are twelve it is the sweet spring.

The briar, the briar she grows up above,
Where no one may pick her to give to their love,
She grows—oh she grows—all so sweet as any rose,
And sweetly she smells when that Summer is close.

The apples, the apples a-hanging so red,
A-bending the branches that bow overhead,
They grow—oh they grow—and are sweet to the tongue,
Apples, fine apples, when September be young.

The Holly, the holly a-shining to sight,
His leaves they do glisten, his berries be bright,
He grows—oh he grows—at the ending of the year,
To cheer our housen when that Kirsmas be here.

NOTE   The first verse contains a reference to the old Somerset saying,
'If you can put your foot on twelve daisies at once Spring has really come.'
    In the last verse Holly is referring to Holly-boy. Holly is always
masculine.
    We children sang this calendar-dance in Calmington Meadows form-
ing a slow circle with an in-and-out walking step and swinging of arms.

5

William Webber

Groom, aged 70, Tangier, Taunton, 1904–1909

Everybody called him 'William' though his surname was Webber and I think even he had forgotten it—but step into the stable-yard down in Tangier and call, 'William', and there he was beside you as noiselessly and nimbly as a bird. His thin legs in long, shiny leggings made him look like one too, and he was a small, quick man with a bright eye. Someone described him as 'dapper and spry as a Robin Herdick' and it fitted his neat, noiseless movements and his perpetual tuneful whistling of airs dear to my soul. He was a wonderful hand with horses—they loved him nearly as much as I did; he had a clear, fluty voice for a good song, and sang it, and his fund of rhozzums[1] and folk-tales was a well of humour that never ebbed, and left his hearers laughing, as they still do sixty years after.

His only grievance was that there were so few songs about horses—hunting, yes, but actual horses—no. He had tried his hand at turning out one himself but could never find the right tune for it. It was of the true folk song stuff and began:

> The huntsman rides a black horse,
> The soldier rides a grey.
> To come and go
> And plough and mow
> And 'Hup' and 'Wo!'
> I'll buy a bonny bay.

[1] Rhozzum—a short funny tale.

23

which I loved. But he never sang it the same way twice, which was terribly frustrating; and then to comfort me he would lose himself and me, too, in following the history of 'Old Tom'.

[TUNE EIGHT]

THERE GOES OLD TOM

Sung by William Webber, Tangier, Taunton, 1906.

There was an old pony just twelve hands high.
Hard away, hark away, there goes Old Tom.
His muzzle was mealy with a nice toad-eye[1].
Over, hup over!
Over, hup over!
He'd hunt all out over but never in vain.
Hard away, hark away, there goes Old Tom.
And bring Farmer home in the fog and the rain.
Over, out over!
Over, out over!
At wall or water when hounds did run on,
Over or under or through went Old Tom.
Over, hup over!
Hard away, hark away, there goes Old Tom.

He'd trot on to market and think it was play,
And bring missus safe to the end of the day.
He'd carry the baby so sweet as a song,
But he hadn't a minute for them as was wrong.

---

[1] Toad-eye—the light ringed eye of a true Exmoor pony.

For his heels went up and his head it went down,
And he'd kick 'en so nicely right down to the town.

They both of 'en died the same day it was said,
And farmer's in churchyard among his dear dead.
They laid the old pony in Ten Acre Mow.
'Twas kind in old Tommy to help it to grow.
With his mealy nose and his titupping toes,
The ponies still follow wherever he goes.
His ghost leads 'en on with cunning and care,
Out away over from Bampton Fair.

We started at a fine lick, and grew slower with each verse until after the last one the silence drew on, to be broken by my subdued sniffs, and it was high time for a rhozzum that made me shriek with laughter.

He was not a religious man, he once told me gravely—to anyone who worked with horses 'language flowed'—but as a country lad he had learned and remembered one Bible tale and he forthwith fluted 'Old Mother Eve' with a perfectly grave face, and thin legs tilted apart like the robin he so resembled.

NOTE   There is a tradition that 'Old Tom' the pony ghost takes the herds away before the round-ups. He is sometimes heard above Chetsford Bridge calling a warning and ponies scatter at once.

'Old' is a term of affection but is also used politely with reference to the Other World.

A pony is a general term for any horse from hunter to cart-horse.

[TUNE NINE]

OLD MOTHER EVE

Sung by William Webber, Tangier, Taunton, 1906.

The apple tree stood in the garden
Its blossoms as white as the snow, the snow,
And there in the cool of the evening,
Our dear Lord God He did go, He did go.

But Old Mother Eve she liked apples
And Adam he liked 'en too, he liked 'en too, he liked 'en too.

The Serpent he hid in the garden
A-twined about the tree, the tree.
'Yew never did eat of such wonderful meat
And so honey sweet.' said he, he, he.

But Old Mother Eve she liked apples
And Adam he liked 'en too, he liked 'en too, he liked 'en too.

They turned 'en both out of the garden
Shut out with a fiery key, key, key,
But Old Man Adam he rolled up his sleeves
And planted an apple-tree, tree, tree.

But Old Mother Eve she liked apples
And Adam he liked 'en too, he liked 'en too, he liked 'en too.

There are apple-trees down in the garden
There are orchets in valley below, below.

26

In autumn and spring the apple is king
And we bless it wherever we go, go, go.

For Old Mother Eve she liked apples
And Adam he liked 'en too, he liked 'en too, he liked 'en too.

NOTE   This is one of the many wassail songs sung round the open-fire on Catterns Eve and New Year's Eve but *not* on Twelfth Night, as the Twelfth Night wassailling is addressed to the pagan tree-spirits, and the guardians of the orchard, and any mention of God would drive them away.

6

Two Aunties and a Great-Great-Granny

Aunt Thurza Bond, Taunton Deane, 1920's

Granny Criddle, Frome Selwood, 1920's

Aunt Loveday Blackmore, Ashbrittle area,

died 1962, aged 80

I never met either of these Aunties and am indebted to Mrs. Strong of Holford Farm and Mrs. Lewis of Lawford Farm for their vivid memories of known local singers. 'Aunt' Thurza came from somewhere in Taunton Deane and used to come to tea-parties at the house of an old lady friend near French Weir, and their great joy was to get together at the piano and sing tinkly Victorian ditties of the 1870's. Among her songs, however, were some much older, and she and Great-great-granny Criddle of Frome Selwood always sang one—'The Lily she grows in the Greenwood'. Mrs. Strong remembers her well. 'We children used to go to Granny's just to listen to them singing. Aunt Thurza, as we called her, was a thin, little old lady. I can still see her. She always wore black with black beads, and her hair was pulled back tight with wispy bits sticking out—dry and thin as old peoples' hair is; and she stood up very straight and warbled away in a weak old voice.'

[TUNE TEN]

THE BRIAR AND THE OAKEN TREE

Sung by Aunt Thurza Bond and her friends, Taunton, 1913.

SHE: Oh if I were a red, red briar and you were an oaken tree,
           I'd twine all about and blossom for thee.
           You'd hold me so closely my one and only dear,
BOTH: And we'd live and we'd love for a hundred year.

HE: If you were a red, red briar and I were an oaken tree,
           I'd cherish they blossoms so sweet they 'ood be.
           I'd hold 'ee so closely, my very own dear,
BOTH: And we'd live and we'd love for a hundred year.

Aunt Thurza Bond always sang 'The Lily She Grows in the Green-wood' as well. So apparently did my East Somerset farmer's widow of ninety, Great-great-granny Criddle, about whom I received several letters and finally the song itself. It was her only

NOTE   This is one of the Old Shepherd's songs, possibly popularized, or else derived from some very early Victorian ballad. He used to sing it to himself in the farm kitchen when I was tiny. One indication that the duet may be Jacobean in origin is the strong tradition adhering to it. It may not be sung by the young, and is regarded as the song of the old who are happily married. ''Tisn't wise vor 'ee to sing that. Yew two wait till you've a-reached our years with the help of God.' This reproof came from two seventy-year-old grannies after an engaged couple sang it at a village concert .They thought to give pleasure but were received in dead silence, and everyone anxiously waited for the engagement to be broken off. As my friend is now awaiting her Golden Wedding she can sing it with village approval whenever she likes.

song and she always sang it on every possible social occasion. She was a massive old lady and to hear her singing a child's funeral ditty at harvest supper must have been startling—but everyone took it in their stride and joined lustily in the choruses because it was Great-great-granny's song and, therefore, highly popular.

I have also heard that it was beloved and sung near Churchinford on the Blackdown Hills up to 1960; but I was away at the time and lost that singer. Aunt Loveday Blackmore knew and sang another version of it.

[TUNE ELEVEN]

THE LILY SHE GROWS IN THE GREENWOOD

Sung in Taunton Deane, Frome Selwood and Blackdown Hills, 1890–1960.

> *The Lily she grows in the Greenwood,*
> *Maidens, maidens, take care!*
> *Her sweet-scented breath do tell your death*
> *Maidens beware!*

There were once a little young maid
Pluck't 'en for her mother;
In the spring when birds do sing,
Died afore another.

Four fair maidens all in white
Carried her a-weeping
Four white kerchiefs bore her up
To her early sleeping.

All a-white the child did go
All so white as winter snow

30

Bunch of lilies to her breast
To show she died a maiden.

Brides may wear them in their crown
Going to their wedding,
Maidens they do lay adown
Wives arise from bedding.

Aunt Loveday Blackmore who died in the 1960's near Ashbrittle
was for most of her life in demand as a singer at farm supper
parties, when the neighbours came in from all round and someone
brought a fiddle or a mouth organ, and the company sat round the
great open fire in the farm kitchen and the old songs went the
rounds. No gramophones or wireless then, and a good tune was
handed on and cherished and a new song was tested out and

NOTE   In this interesting old account of a child's funeral and the superstitions surrounding the death of a maiden, there is a break-away from
the universal dread of the snowdrop——'Take a bunch of snowdrops
into the house and the girl child will die in the year.'

The old also show affront if given snowdrops—'Be 'ee trying to
hasten my coffin?' or 'Sewing my shroud already?'—but here the lily of
the valley is viewed with suspicion. It may be that as they are also
regarded as flowers to heal the heart—they are still in veterinary use
and extremely good—they were, as plants of the earth, too potent for
unwary maids to wear. To wives and mothers they were quite friendly
and healthful.

The heavily scented white narcissus 'Eggs and butter' and white lilac
are both regarded as unlucky to the unmarried. I have known them
refused houseroom particularly where there is an invalid, unless, as in
many hospitals, they are mixed with coloured blooms.

Granny Criddle was over ninety, an old age pensioner, a widow and
a great-great-granny, when she last sang this at a wedding in 1921.

discarded as Market Street rubbish, or carefully retained and brought out regularly because it told a good tale like 'The Goose-feather Bed'.

[TUNE TWELVE]

THE GOOSE-FEATHER BED

Sung by Aunt Loveday Blackmore, Ashbrittle Area, 1890's, and by ballad singers at Taunton Market, 1830's to 1850's.

Young Jenny she sat all a-weeping,
For both her dear parents were dead.
The larder was bare and no money was there,
All she had was a goose-feather bed.

Jack's mother she sent him a-courting,
But soon he came back and he said,
'She's all skin and bone, so I'll leave her alone,
For who wants a goose-feather bed?'

Tom Higgler came looking for bargains,
The house was quite bare, so he said,
'Now listen, young Jenny, I'll give you one penny
To purchase the goose-feather bed.'

Young Jenny she sat there a-weeping,
When Richard the Farmer rode up;
'Come, lass, we'll be wed. I've a use for your bed,
When you've eaten a good bite and sup.'

But Young Jack and Tom they went laughing;
To the countryside round they both said,

32

'What a bargain he got with that raggedy lot!
What use is a goose-feather bed?'

At the end of the year they met Farmer,
With his pretty wife arm in crook,
And a nice little son, and everyone run
To see how these jokers would look.

For Jenny was happy and handsome,
And her cloak it was warm and red.
Said Farmer, 'My missus do thrive upon kisses,
There's Luck in a Goose-feather bed.'

She was also a fine leading 'diddler', singing and clapping time to
dancers in kitchens and barns or harvest fields where there were
no musicians, or they were quenching their thirsts with cider.
The most popular barn dance tunes were 'Brighton Camp' or
'Abram Brown', but Aunt Loveday's words are worthy of a place
in folk music.

[TUNE THIRTEEN]

I TOOK MY DAME TO LAMBING FEAST

*Words sung to the air 'Abram Brown', and used for diddling at barn
dances, Ashbrittle area, 1903.*

I took my Dame to lambing feast,
We all sat down to supper.
The table tipped and down she slipped,
A-rolling in the butter.
But up she got and ate the lot
While we were all a flutter.

She golloped a barrel of cider brew,
So I carted her home on a shutter.

The shutter crack and a-broke in half,
And I fell over the cat;
While all the neighbours they did laugh
To see a thing like that.
They stuck her up on pig-sty roof,
Oh, what a thing to do!
For she were in the flower of her youth,
She was but one hundred and two!

NOTE I have helped 'diddle' with the older women on the hayfields and in a barn when the dancers stood up. We kept the rhythm with clapping and stamping to our singing. The two most used tunes were 'Brighton Camp' and 'Abram Brown'. Occasionally we used some of 'Old Shepherd's'. Like William Winter the Bagborough fiddler, his tunes were regarded as his own property and have been lost at his death. They both had large repertoires.

7

Annie's Granny

Farm maid and then charwoman, born Taunton
Vale, 1834, died Almshouse, Chard area, 1922

Annie's Granny had no name: she had no right to one for she was
a 'chance-come' (the innocent result of a rape in a lonely lane,
perpetrated by some passing 'Itinerant'). Her mother was just
thirteen. However, her mother's parents gave both the shelter of
their roof, which was all they dare do in the face of countryside
rulings, and, again according to rural codes of behaviour, saw that
they both 'worked for it'. This serfdom was rewarded by a kind
small corner in the community, free of hard names and words,
very unlike the hordes of little hose-birds (whore's brood)[1] who
later on crowded the Taunton courts near the barracks, and whose
lady mammas assiduously 'followed the drum'. Those poor children never met with any reaction but public comments on their
mother's past and their own prison futures, and rewarded an
unexpected kindly word or act with a stare of defiance, and, when
at a safe distance from pursuit, with carefully selected bespatter-
ings of dung. Annie's Granny, however, was allowed to maintain
her self-respect by working for it, and was fiercely self-reliant and
never let her hands lie idle. She began work when toddling beside her little mother and picking the rushes which her mother

1 Somerset pronunciation showing typical reversion of aspirates—

bird—breed
brood
hose—whore's

35

peeled, dipped in a clay mould of melted tallow (used again and again) and tied into meagre bundles at a farthing a rushlight, which they trudged into Taunton to sell at the doors of the weavers' cottages. Sometimes they brought home a whole penny to prove their working worth while. This was such a worthy matter that at fifteen her mother was married to an elderly farm labourer who permitted the 'chance-come' room under his thatched roof and whatever food there was to be shared, and in all her life never spoke to her. He was a good, kind man, and she and her mother were considered fortunate and returned such kindness by a weekly amount of work which would keep a dozen modern factory workers employed over a month. At five she was minding and teaching her young brother (Annie's grandfather) to go 'leasing corn' with mother, who now had a smaller daughter toddling at her skirts, a babe in her shawl, and another on the way. The leasings of such little beings all helped to fill a small bag to be ground into meal for porridge. They were too poor to spare even the cup-full that miller would dip out for his payment. They ground their own—each little tot banging away with a stone upon the flat rock that the measter[1] had placed as a threshold, doorstep or chopping block leading into their thatched, single-roomed home. The measter had built it on a waste corner of land—raising its walls of cob, throwing bracken thatch over its rafters, and lighting his fire on an open hearth all in the one day, as custom allowed. Henceforth by squatters' right he owed no man rent, and the saving of one shilling a week was immense, and even assisted towards keeping a pig to sell, in search of scraps for whom small feet toiled weary miles. Annie's Granny fed the pig and the two hens that Farmer's wife had meant to kill because they ailed, until Annie's Granny begged for them and cured them with her ever

[1] Measter—see Anthony Munday Coney Catcher Bod. mss. Tudor Maister—master.

36

watchful ways, and then sometimes there were eggs to be sold too. She minded the growing family, taking them in all weathers to gather the stones in heaps from Farmer's fields, and fill up his rutted roadways with them; she took them out to the paddocks while the farm-men mended gaps in the hedges, and let the little things roll and trot about on the grass so long as they watched where cows or sheep were straying, her own six-year-old fingers busily sorting and turning their flower gatherings into bunches of white violets or primroses bound with a bit of grass to be sold in Taunton for a whole penny each. Not that she ever owned a penny herself: the 'chance-come' paid its way for leave to live, and all life's pleasures until she died at eighty-eight were only the joys of looking and learning. Even so she found time to sing to the family, to tell old tales up in the cock-loft and, if asked by Farmer's own brood, to teach them the old dances she had sat and watched from her dark corner. During the years, in his scant leisure time, the measter had added a cock-loft above the straw-filled box bed. It was reached by pegs driven up the wall and the growing brood of chicks were roosted there to work and sleep. By the time she was just eight she had taught other little fingers to peel and plait withies into little toy egg-baskets, and to plait rush-hats and weave rush-mats of the 'levvers' growing in the streams, to tie up water-cresses and sing their song to gain customers; and Farmer's wife considered she 'could make a useful little maid of she'.

The cock-loft up the peg ladder was crowded, if warm, and there would be more for all to eat if she and Annie's grandfather, now six, went out into the world—he to earn his penny a week as carter's boy, sleeping comfortably in the straw under the manger of his giant charges and having stale crusts in plenty, and even a sup of milk which had not to be shared with an avid brood of young ones. Annie's Granny, too, saw good rough food handed to her—even such delicacies as bread and scrapings of pig lard and skim

milk or whey in a tin cup. And she worked harder than ever—
here, there, all around the place like the pixies she loved to tell
about, and looking not unlike a strayed one herself for she never
grew larger than an eleven-year-old.

She never saw her money; it was always paid to her mother.
Even when at thirteen she bettered herself by 'going scullery
maid' to the Hall, and then at fourteen sole maid-servant to a
Taunton tradesman, she still had nothing for herself. It was not
until her worn-out mother died at the age of twenty-eight, leaving
a family of fourteen, at least six of whom had yet to begin earning,
that the young maid-servant's wages were reckoned to be her own
at last.

Not for this 'chance-come'.

They were spent on keeping an eye on the half-dozen orphans
and their silent old father, on visits bringing rare odds and ends of
broken farm meats, and out-grown mended Taunton children's
clothes, and above all on boots. But even meagre regular wages
last over the years, and the brood took wing and flew to the jobs
she found for them: weeding-boy at the Hall, bird-scarers at the
farms, stocking knitters and little 'tween maids in local homes. If
she asked for a place for them it was given. She had taught them
all to work for their bread, and their old father was highly
esteemed by his own master. Then at twenty-one there came a
day when the brood had gone, and the old man died quietly while
sleeping at the noon-break in the hay-harvest, and the funeral was
decently over and done with. The 'chance-come' was free to buy
something for her own pleasure. As a sign of entering upon her
own home life, though it might be in someone else's kitchen, she
bought a spotted china cat which cost an entire sixpence, and was
a bargain because its mate had got broken and it had a chip by its
tail. I knew that china cat for twenty-five years. It always stood on
her kitchen mantelpiece with the chip neatly out of sight. It was
with her in the almshouse when she died after another sixty years

of dauntless battling with other people's problems and of disregarding her own, in the never-ending river of work life always found for her. And with it all she found time to memorize, while busy with the washtub, and to sing to us while ironing piles of family laundry for prosperous Taunton citizens, and to find an excuse for neat footwork as we danced single file behind her stamping down a cinder path, singing as we stamped. By now the love of her scattered family for her was trying to make life easier for her and it is from this time the old title of her serfdom faded. Her brother was, like his own father, a kind but voiceless soul, but in the pride and joy of his early marriage and fatherhood found by some miracle a time and place to give tongue to an idea he had worked on for years. His small daughter was called Annie, and in future he solidly and relentlessly spoke of his family's good angel as 'Annie's Granny'. It didn't matter that she wasn't and never could be—it was meant as a brotherly joke, his only one, and the family, slowly chuckling, followed his lead. By the time his Annie grew up and had the Annie I knew and played with, the clan was unanimous, and would have repaid her fine devotion a thousandfold. She could have been extremely comfortable but she preserved her fierce independence and went on working till she died. What she did with her earnings no one enquired—there were always 'grand-sons' and 'grand-daughters' who were starting life, and a little went a long way in those days. Her brothers did insist on handing over the rent-free cottage with its bit of garden and pig sty. They re-thatched it, and turned the cock-loft into a minute bedroom up a cupboard stair, knocked out two windows in the gable-ends and one beside the door, white-washed the whole tiny place inside and out, mended and painted her pig sty and palings, dug over her potato patch for her and planted it, put in three currant bushes, black, white and red, and made her free of her very own home at last. The first thing to go into that house was the china cat; and there it sat through all the years of singing and endless sewing, rag-rugmaking (from the wreckage of 'grand-sons'' trousers) and rhozzums and folk tales. How to cure a ring-worm with a foxglove leaf, how to summon the wraith of a future lover in silence on one of the wisht nights, how to coax a proud parsley plant to grow in your garden plot on the right day, what to wish when the first cuckoo called, and why May-born horses were not to be trusted; the china cat heard all these and hundreds more.

In later years, I came to the cottage to visit and sing while she sat briskly shelling peas, mending a tear in my riding coat or even firmly re-stitching all my coat buttons, and darning the finger tips of string gloves to ensure a good grip on wet leathers. At the end of each song or tale she might give a sharp nod of approval, but no more. In spite of her small size she was a daunting little person, sharp-tongued, sharp-eared and sharp-eyed, with a devastating knowledge which was absolutely accurate. And yet children and family loved her and I counted the hours lost in my precious quarter century that I couldn't contrive somehow to visit her, and be well cut down to size. She had known me all my life so when the end was near the family got word to me. The cottage was empty (Annie herself and the china cat had it later) and I went to a South Somerset almshouse just opposite the farm of a favou-rite 'great-grandson'. I went into the tiny, dark bed-sittingroom and there was Annie's Granny reaching out a thin, shaky idle hand to me, and there was the china cat gazing at me from the mantel-piece. 'There be summat I want to sing to 'ee, my dear', said the weak old voice. 'The time have come for they to be passed on to the Right One.' She had known all my life that I was a Chime Child and this was her first and only direct reference to it.

Out of her vast lore she knew the two 'fairy songs' would be in safe and loving hands and she could relinquish her guardianship of treasures belonging to Those Others. She sang them to me in a tired thread of a voice—and because of her age and infinite weakness the haunting tunes are rather alike, but I sang them back to her as she lay sunk in the pillows and listened.

When I finished she gave my hand a squeeze and said, 'That'll be all, then', and I got up and went away, first carefully turning the china cat to hide the crack more neatly.

[TUNE FOURTEEN]

THE SPUNKY

Sung by Annie's Granny, Blackdown Hills, 1922.

The Spunky he went like a sad little flame,
All, all alone.
All out on the zogs[1] and a-down the lane,
All, all alone.
A tinker came by that was full of ale,
And into the mud he went head over tail,
All, all alone.

A crotchety Farmer came riding by,
All, all alone.
He cursed him low and he cursed him high,
All, all alone.
The Spunky he up and he led him astray,
The pony were foundered until it were day,
All, all alone.

There came an old Granny—she see the small Ghost,
All, all alone.

1 zog—marshland.

'Yew poor liddle soul all a-cold, a-lost,
All, all alone.
I'll give 'ee a criss-cross to save 'ee bide;
Be off to the Church and make merry inside,
All, all alone.'

The Spunky he laughed ,'Here I'll galley[1] no more!'
All, all alone.
And off he did wiver[2] and in at the door,
All, all alone.
The souls they did sing for to end his pain,
There's no little Spunky a-down the lane,
All, all alone.

[TUNE FIFTEEN]

COLD LIES THE DEW

Sung by Annie's Granny, Blackdown Hills, 1922.

There was an old Granny who lost her sight,
Cold lies the Dew.
She couldn't tell if it were morning or night,
Cold lies the Dew.

NOTE   A Spunky is the ghost of an unbaptised babe, a will o' the wisp.
It leads travellers to water in the forlorn hope that they will christen
it—'Give it a criss-cross.' Once named it may join the Christian dead in
church. In West and South Somerset turnip lanterns representing the
dead are shown at Hallows-tide and known as Punkies. To sing of a
ghost (unless gifted) was to risk raising them.

[1] galley—scare.   [2] wiver—waver and quiver.

There come a fine gentleman, black as a coal,
'I'll give 'ee some eyes, if you'll sell me your soul,'
Cold lies the Dew.

Singing
Green, green, green, all a-green, all a-green,
A-dancing round the Tree.

She gave him a criss-cross, she muttered a prayer,
Cold lies the Dew.
And off with a scritch he went up in the air,
Cold lies the Dew.
The poor old Granny she longed for her eyes,
And down on her knees goes her head and she cries,
Cold lies the Dew.

There came a pit-patter and Somebody says,
Cold lies the Dew.
'All your long life you've a-minded our ways,
Cold lies the Dew.
With pail of spring water and cream bowl too'—
They led her away in the May morning dew,
Cold lies the Dew.

Her sight came back, it was clear and fine,
Cold lies the Dew.
Her pretty blue eyes they was all a-shine,
Cold lies the Dew.
She stood all alone there—Then who were 'They'?
The wise old Granny she never would say,
Cold lies the Dew.

NOTE The exceedingly ancient horn refrain to this song dates the original words as right back in time. The present words are eighteenth century or even later, built on and including older ones. This is a purely magical song only known among 'the gifted' since it speaks so freely of fairy lore. Even so, the naming of unchancy beings is carefully avoided. It is commonplace even now to call them 'They'. 'They been and a-hid my ball of wool up in the tallat.' The Tree is the hawthorn that grows on the fairy mound, the gateway to the unseen world.

This song can be compared with 'The Hawthorn Tree Bride' and 'The Garland of Clay', both Somerset Folk Songs.

8

Richard Garland, the Sedgemoor Soldier

Born about 1895, down by the withy country,

killed in action in France, 1917

My very beloved younger brother had been killed at Gallipoli and I had been sent away on a visit to distract my grief. Where I was staying in the Midlands there was one of the many small hospitals for convalescing wounded, so soon to be sent back into the necessity and nightmare of the Flanders Front.

It was a daily occurence to see the blue-clad men hobbling and halting about neighbouring houses, their pale faces cheerfully challenging their scarlet ties. Everyone made them welcome and tried to put aside thoughts of their grim future, and I helped, not too successfully.

Some of these very men had been invalided home two or three times, to be returned to France to fill up the ranks of skeleton battalions often composed of the survivors of a dozen county regiments.

'Coo! some perishers cop it real lucky', said one cheerful cockney. 'Old Dick Garland there catches three proper Blightys, one arter annuver, didn't he, mates? Now they're chucking him back in again to cop another. Arter being three times lucky, poor cove. Ow! it's a luvly war!'

Old Dick Garland must have been about twenty-one, but his wounds and weariness made him even more silent than the usual countryman.

He was very tall and angular-boned and had a face rough-hewn out of stone. He was abysmally shy and was always planted right at the very back of every group, listening, but never one of the party, his long, slow, slouching stride somehow contriving to keep time with their pride in being able to march smartly if only as far as a corner, hiding their weakness from too kind hosts.

I recognized that slouch and was drawn to it out of my own sorrows, and sought an opportunity to break the icy barrier of silence.

It came when a short outing on foot to more hospitality was arranged. My friends, surrounding the Cockneys and Welsh and Northern invalids, moved on in an aura of cheerful laughter and jokes and I dragged behind. Behind me even further slouched the silent Dick Garland. And then he broke silence, quietly and sweetly singing to himself, and my homesickness and heartache vanished at this exiled Somerset voice. I stood waiting for him to catch up, and, hearing the ominous ditty he sang and sighting the shadow I had seen before, knew why he was singing at all. He spoke without preamble, ''Twon't do 'ee no harm to hear, miss.' So he had recognized a Chime Child—perhaps he was one himself. ' 'Tis one of they old songs not always lucky to the singer.' 'What part of Sedgemoor do you hail from?' I asked. The shadow lifted a moment. 'There's withy beds down whoame and one of my grandads lives Shapwick way. Do 'ee know Levvers Water Farm?' he went on with sudden eagerness; then the silence and shadow fell again. He wouldn't be seeing it again, any more than my dear brother would visit the Exmoor he loved and always planned to retire to in our old age; but we journeyed on slowly in a companionable silence, my pace matching his moorman's heavy stride, and presently found ourselves singing the Sedgemoor lament.

46

[TUNE SIXTEEN]

ON SEDGEMOOR (THE MARSH FEVER)

Sung by Richard Garland near Birmingham, Autumn, 1917.

When the mist be all about,
Then let no man venture out.
It will grip you, hale or stout,
Without doubt.
For death he is a-walking, a-walking, a-walking,
For to find his dead,
And the marish ground do shiver to his tread.
Lie safe a-bed!

When the mist lies low before,
You may set your cottage door,
You may labour on the moor
Safe and sure.
For Death is gone a-walking, a-walking, a-walking,
For to find his dead,
And the marish ground do shiver to his tread,
But the sun be overhead.

We caught up and were engulfed in the lights and hospitality
of the group, and were separated. Later I caught a glimpse of him,

NOTE   It is believed on Sedgemoor that the mist kills any man who
tries to work in it unless it is only knee high.

This was one of Isaiah Sully's tantalizing fragments but I got the whole
song from one of my sexton clan from near Wedmore. He said it was
sung near Othery in his youth.

47

standing, as usual, well back in a corner, and, catching my eye, he raised a shy forefinger to his forelock in country greeting and appreciation.

The last party for the convalescents was a terrifically jolly affair. They were to sail tomorrow and I prised Dick Garland from a lonely corner behind a potted palm-plant and found a window-seat in which he might once more sing to solace our heartaches for a too distant Somerset. ''Tis a bit of old lost song but there's withies in it,' he managed to say.

[TUNE SEVENTEEN]

LANGPORT TOWN OR THE WATER WITCH

The refrain sung by Richard Garland near Birmingham, Autumn 1917.

By the beds of green withies a young man I espied,
Lamenting his true love, lamenting his bride.

All on a summer morning she went to Langport town,
But she never comed home again, she never comed home again,
She never comed home again, when the moon it went down.
Oh Ellum do grieve, and Oak he do hate,
But Willow, Willow, Willow,
Willow do walk if you travel late.

By the beds of green withies when morning did arise
He found his dear Nanny, all a-drownèd she lies.

All on a summer morning she went to Langport Town, etc.

48

'I have lost my dearest Nanny,' he sobbed and he cried
'Afloating down river, all a-drift on the tide,'

All on a summer morning she went to Langport Town, etc.

He only knew the chorus, but he sang and I sang too, very quietly, and then we were collected in for a rowdy sing-song and then the men had to go. The air was loaded with thanks and jokes, and as ever he was the last to go.

He turned shyly in the doorway and said, 'Well, goodnight all,' and went, and the shadow was over him as he did.

He was killed in France within the week.

Years later, I was sitting with a cheerful Exmoor farmhouse group all enjoying an evening's singing of songs—mine and theirs, old and new, but mostly the songs of tradition. A farmer uncle seated on the settle listened to them in silence and when at last we desisted for a moment from sheer exhaustion he rose and made a slow way to the door for his long moorland road homewards. In the doorway he paused in his going, 'My boy he knowed all they old songs—ah—and a good many more—*but he never come back.* Well—goodnight all.' We sang no more that night. The shadow had descended on the folk-singers of a whole generation, and we that were left had a sadly empty treasury.

NOTE   Richard Garland only remembered the refrain with its reference to the tidal river Parret turning herself into a water-witch willow, and strangling and drowning belated travellers, like the tree near Cromford beside the River Derwent in Derbyshire.

The whole song seems to have been forgotten for over a century. A Muchelney woman who had been transported to Australia became the nurse to an overseer's household. She taught the song when a very old woman to her charges, and one of them asked his grandchildren to send it to me after his death.

It returned to Somerset from Australia about 1950.

9

Delilah Odcombe

Family servant in her 70's, South Somerset, 1920's

Her elderly mistress was a permanent invalid with a puckish sense of humour that sparkled through the painfully scrawled letters which I received over a period of three years.

Delilah had been the family servant all their lives. They were both old and went from Somerset town to village and on again in search of interest and alleviation of pain until the end came.

I never heard where or when; the letters just stopped.

The mistress wrote, 'I shall call her Delilah Odcombe to you. We Somerset people resent our own names being mentioned to strangers. I laughed a lot when I made it up. If you could see her you'd laugh too.' Later letters gave flashes of vivid description, large, bounteous, flat-footed and moon-faced. 'A face like a currant bun', wrote her mistress, 'with two currants for eyes, and someone had cut a knife slit for the mouth. My brother the Vicar has always been scared of her since he was a little boy.'

She must have dominated that clerical household, tremendous of size and decisions, and also of voice. She loved singing but as a Christian ecclesiastical servant deprived herself of it until she found solace in doing so shut away in her kitchen. That the whole house reverberated never entered her head; no one was supposed to know anything about the songs. They only existed behind a firmly closed kitchen door. They were not 'they sinful folk songs that they do call them, that people sing all about here', they were religious! That is to say, they contained some Biblical reference and therefore became acceptable under a clerical roof.

She sang this haunting old song of Mary Magdalene blissfully unaware that her voice and words through an open kitchen window went rolling and echoing right down the village street. It was heard and noted by a keen folklorist and passed on to me years later.

[TUNE EIGHTEEN]

MARY MAGDALENE

Sung by Delilah Odcombe, Martock to Yeovil area, 1920's.

Mary, Mary, Mary Magdalene
She was a whore of Jerusalem.

She wore a green[1] gown, when she laid her a-down
On a bed of pease-straw.[2]

Mary, Mary, Mary Magdalene
She was a whore of Jerusalem.

They bringed[3] her in a band, a stone in every hand
Our Dear Lord afore.

Mary, Mary, Mary Magdalene
She was a whore of Jerusalem.

'You was an honest maid afore you took this trade,
Go—sin no more.'

[1] green—denotes light morals.
[2] pease-straw leaves an unsightly rash.
[3] bringed—brought.

51

Mary, Mary, Mary Magdalene
She was a whore of Jerusalem.

She poured 'en ointment sweet, and her tears did
    dry His feet,
And she wept very sore.

When they went to Watchet, she journeyed on again with a local version of 'Joseph was a Tinner'.

St. Joseph of Arimathea had landed there to trade for metal, so tradition told, but I don't suppose she learned the current children's jingles:

You'm a liard![1] You'm a sinner!
Sure as Joseph was a Tinner.

and the local reference to a shallow Severn Sea:

Joseph was a tinner
He sailed his little boat
He come ashore at Watchet
'Cause he couldn't keep afloat.

Another version of the song is to be found somewhere among Mendip miners, but the tune is now lost.

NOTE   One old man I knew went to see a fine stained glass window in the church and came back disgruntled—'All they weeping womenfolk round the Cross, and they left the poor Magdalene out of it. Not a one in green.' This suggests some tradition about her attire. Green is the fairy colour, and fairy ladies are often wanton lovers.

1 liard—liar.

As they grew old together her mistress persuaded her to alleviate the long pain-wracked hours by singing to her such items in her repertoire as the seventeenth-century 'Eve Was a Fine Ladye' and 'The Twelve Apostles', which is rich in country lore.

[TUNE NINETEEN]

THE TWELVE APOSTLES

Sung by Delilah Odcombe, Somerset 1920's

The twelve apostles they were standing by,
Their roots in the river, and their leaves in the sky,
The beasts all thrive wherever they be,
But Judas was a-hangèd on an elder tree.

The Twelve Apostles in the garden plot do grow,
Some be blue, some be red and others white as snow,
They cure the ill of every man, whatever ill it be,
But Judas he was hangèd on an elder tree.

The twelve apostles they did follow Our Lord,
They journeyed after when he travelled abroad,
But Judas sold him for a silver fee,
Now cursed be Judas let him hang on the tree.

NOTE 'The twelve apostles' is usually the local name for any group of trees surrounding a pool. In verse 2, however, it is the name given to lungwort, which is often called 'Joseph and Mary' elsewhere in the county.

The elder is held as accursed on the Blackdown Hills and along the Severn coast from Steart Point to Watchet: 'Never use elder to your

Since it was a duty Delilah sang (she was all duty) and in spider trail through painful hours the invalid copied down words and airs for me, accompanied by letters that were brief and twinkling. Those letters, alas! were claimed by the blitz, but for one of the last and most hilarious recorded—'Nutting on Sunday'.

'Apparently,' wrote the invalid, 'the mention of a Biblical Devil made it entirely acceptable!'

[TUNE TWENTY]

NUTTING ON SUNDAY

Sung by Delilah Odcombe, Mastock to Yeovil area, 1920's.

> Oh there was a maid, and a foolish young maid,
> And she went a-nutting on Sunday.
> She met with a Gentleman all in black,
> He took and he laid her a-down on her back,
> All a-cause she went nutting on Sunday.
>
> In spite of her moan he took her for his own,
> All a-cause she went nutting on Sunday.
> She was his for ever after—and home she did run
> Lamenting and weeping for maid she was none,
> All a-cause she went nutting on Sunday.

---

fire ('twont burn in Ell vlames cos Judas he were burnded already)'. Many farmers complained about hedge trimmers who refused to tie up elder into faggots, and a popular superstition is still held that if you cut elder it bleeds. This adverse belief is very strange in view of its invaluable assistance in many ways for curative purposes.

At the end of the year her shame was made clear,
All a-cause she went nutting on Sunday.
For the baby did come before the ring,
It had horns and a tail! What a terrible thing!
All a-cause she went nutting on Sunday.

Now all you young maidens take warning by this,
And never go nutting on Sunday.
For the Wicked do lurk to encompass his work,
And if you don't heed him you'll come to no hurt,
So—NEVER GO NUTTING ON SUNDAY!

NOTE   Nutting on Sunday is the equivalent to rush gathering, going maying, and vuzz-laying—all denoting loose behaviour. It was regarded as the sign of a witch initiate, and was shouted after her as an insult.

10

Seafarers from the Severn Sea

(a) *The Three Danish Galleys*

I had just finished a Folk Song Recital in London, and made my way back to sink exhausted into my dressing-room chair, when there came a hearty bang on my door which opened, and an elderly sea captain came in. He was smart, grey-haired, scarlet-faced, and as full of enthusiasm as a young westerly gale—and he had a ballad for me. His family had been Porlock folk right back to Drake's time and before, and they had treasured and kept strictly to themselves this ancient ballad. Now having listened to that evening's Somerset wealth, he had decided regardless of family traditions that it must be brought to the free air of a singing world and that I was the one to do it. Before the force of this Severn Gale, I found my weariness blown clean away, and was soon singing too. He had a tremendous voice and it hit like hammer-blows into my memory. He sailed tomorrow he said, so I must learn it then and now. I did, every verse, and sang it back to him. He gave me a delighted smile, a hearty farewell and a handshake that clamped my fingers for the rest of the evening, and went away, forgetting to leave his name.

The Danish raids on Porlock are mentioned in the Anglo-Saxon Chronicle, and 'The Three Danish Galleys' is a very ancient ballad which has survived the alterations of singers of other centuries, and is surprisingly unspoiled.

[TUNE TWENTY-ONE]

THE THREE DANISH GALLEYS

Sung in London 1919 by a sea captain born in Porlock.

Three galleys come sailing to Porlock Side,
And stole me away a new-wed bride,
Who left my true love lying dead on the shore,
Sailing out and away.
I never shall see my dear home no more.

Then up to her stepped the Danish King,
And her he would wed with a golden ring,
Who left my true love, etc.

The bride she made answer her tears between,
I never will wed with a cowardly Dene.[1]
Who left my true love, etc.

Then out of the galley they tossed the Bride,
And laughed as she drowned in the cruel tide.
Who left my true love, etc.

There came three small galleys from Porlock Bay,
They fought with the Danes for a night and a day.
Who left my true love, etc.

They fought till the decks with blood ran red,
And every man of the Danes was dead.
Who left my true love, etc.

[1] Dene—Dane. Local pronunciation.

Then back into Porlock they towed the Bride,
And buried her down below the Tide.[1]
Who left my true love, etc.

(b) The Lazy Wave

I heard this at the same time as I learned 'Severn No More' and
from the same two fishermen—one was a much older man respectfully called Mr. Elisha by the young man whose name I never knew.
They were both weather-tanned and horny-handed, with the deep
blue eyes 'set in with smutty fingers' found from the Exmoor sea-
board to Portishead—a Celtic heritage—and they worked on the
foreshore near Birnbeck Island. More I cannot fill in—memory is
clouded because both mother and I had been ill at the time, but
having learned and sung 'Severn No More' with them while osten-
sibly helping with nets, I do remember very clearly one flash back
of quiet argument. The younger had made a song of his own—
excellent—and shyly wished to sing it at work—nothing wrong
about singing at work is there? A man should! But here ethical
doubts intervened for it was not a hymn but a love song. 'But 'tis
meant to be sung with respectful delicacy, Mr. Elisha,' pleaded its
eager, but bashful composer, and Mr. Elisha, listening to the slow
incoming tide, reckoned the melody appealed to him, and so we
learned it, and sang it 'with respectful delicacy'.

I have a very hazy recollection of hearing it again one night and
clambering out of bed, pattering bare-foot over cold linoleum and
gazing from my window over a Weston Bay filled with still water
and moon mist, out of which rang far distant voices—but it can
quite easily have been a dream.

[1] In order that her ghost should not walk.

[TUNE TWENTY-TWO]

THE LAZY WAVE

Composed from an old air and sung by a young fisherman and his mate
at Birnbeck, Weston-super-Mare, 1906.

The lazy wave slides over the sand,
My love and I were hand in hand.
It ran till it came where we did stand,
And faded away in the Severn sand.

Oh love that be new runs in on the tide,
But love that be ebbing will never abide.
Like the lazy wave it do fade away,
And leave you alone for ever a day.

The ships they go sail in the Severn Sea
But never a lad looks out for me.
My heart is a-broked, the heart that I gave
Wasted and gone like the lazy wave.

So lonely I wander by Severn Side
Watching and waiting the turn of the tide.
But no one returns for to claim his bride
And the lazy wave it do fade and hide.

For years my own noncomformist training held me from singing
this—just in case it was something a minister's small daughter
might not do—and it had become deep buried by other songs until

NOTE   The composer was lost at sea in the 1914–18 War.

one glorious September day in 1964, when up on Brean Down overlooking a quiet sea creeping shorewards, the whole song threw off the dust of fifty years and became a lovely and loved thing to others.

(c) The Brean Lament

'The Brean Lament' was sent to me by a Mid-Somerset farmer's daughter in the 1930's and I never knew the old singer of this, nor did my correspondent. Nor did he apparently wish anyone to know much about his way of life. He kept himself dourly to himself and worked grimly and methodically for eighteen hours of a farming day for some forty years.

Now the farmer, who told his daughter all this, was an easygoing, cheerful soul with a growing fund of old countryside songs, which he loved and learned and collected at every possible opportunity. Coming home from a successful day's market he was far more pleased by hearing and remembering a ballad singer than by the well-filled bank book he brought home.

On one memorable Harvest Supper the cider was potent and the old labourer broke into a song—a lovely lament from the Severn Coast—and the farmer sat enchanted. He thought his quick memory had retained it all but next morning, anxious to check up, he approached the old farm hand.

But next morning was next morning, and the old fellow obstinately knew nothing—remembered nothing—until sighting the real disappointment on his master's face, and he was devoted to him, he growled, 'I been shipwrecked five times, ah! And come whoame safe tew—but no-one don't never sing he. 'Tis bad luck!' And was henceforth silent for another twenty years.

[TUNE TWENTY-THREE]
THE BREAN LAMENT

Sung by a farm-hand, an ex-sailor of about fifty, at Caryland, Mid-Somerset, 1900.

> The waters they washed 'en ashore, ashore,
> And they never will sail the seas no more.
> We laid 'en along by the churchyard wall
> And all in a row we buried them all.
> But their boots we buried below the tide
> On Severn Side.
>
> The gulls they fly over so high, so high
> To see where their bodies all safe do lie
> They fly all around and loud they do call
> Where all in a row we buried them all.
> But their boots we buried below the tide
> On Severn Side.

NOTE   The bodies of the drowned at Brean were not buried in the church but on the tide-line until the 1870's, and even when accorded Christian burial were never brought into the Church itself but buried in the Sailors' Graveyard—the sea might wish to reclaim them!

That this lament is regarded as uncanny is natural folk belief. Having the souls of drowned sailors as its theme, and the prevention of 'walking ghosts' by burial where the sea doesn't have to reach out to reclaim its own, it is considered unwise to remind and invite either sea-gulls or Severn to further drownings.[1]

According to estuary lore a sea-gull will attack an exhausted swimmer who is still managing to escape his fate, out of sheer envy of the living. In many western coasts it was the practice even in days of more Christian funerals to bury the boots of the dead on the tide-line. This caused quite a legal upset in the Arran Murder of 1889 as the missing boots were vital evidence.

1 Americal naval belief. See 'Three Years Behind the Guns.' St. Nicholas 1907.

11

Mrs. Cordelia Cooper

A gipsy singer, Exmoor, 1942–3

During the darkest days of World War II, I was away on remote
Exmoor where the air-raid siren of our coastal town, sounded by
accident *once* in four years, provided many months' talk to the
moor farmers.

Away from the coastline and the giant American troops (mainly
Wisconsin and Oregon lumberjacks) it was quite easy to lose
oneself in the ancient silence of the hills—a silence that absorbed
the whisper of wind over hill grasses, the hum of bees in the
heather, the quiet calling of upland birds and the cold tinkle of
little brown streams on their way seaward. It was a perfect place
for a pony to travel, and a perfect place to lift one's voice freely
in old songs which my pony and I enjoyed with an abandonment
which was one with wind and hill-crests and distant silver sea.

Riding and singing through twisting paths in oak woodlands
that clung to the slanted cleeve, always with the sound of a stream
far below, was sheer joy, and so, riding thus, we came one day
upon a very old gipsy woman seated comfortably on the bank-side
in a springy cushion of worts, smoking her pipe, her dusty battered boots stretched before her, and her heavy basket beside her
in yet another clump of short, heavily freighted wortleberries.

The pony pulled up short, and she eyed him like a hawk— trust
a gipsy, and a possible Cooper and that, to find the horse-flesh of
more interest than the rider, so she eyed the pony with growing
satisfaction and I was able to eye her at leisure.

She was not a local Romany—neither Holland, nor Lock. By

the way she eyed the pony she was probably a Cooper out-branch, or a Heron driven far afield by military areas, and camping in the open friendly silences of Exmoor. She was very old and her thin, hawk face under manifold plaits was a fine network of wrinkles, but her voice when she spoke had a harsh resonance and deep music, which I had heard before far below in woods where the wort pickers laboured with bent backs and stained fingers. The voice down in the distant trees had been a part of the solitude and so was the air it sang, and now here she was.

She removed her pipe and lifted a keen gaze to my face. 'Yew do sing so tuneable as the dear God's small birds,' she approved. 'Do 'ee have any knowledge of The Cold, Cold Sea? 'Tis a notable and beautiful song, love.'

I did. So we sang it together while the pony sampled the nearest and juiciest young twigs of worts bushes. We sang more and more, capping each other's, until even the Exmoor pony could eat no more and stood drowsily listening to the steady flow of melodies that extended for over three hours, in the warmth and dappled sunlight of Worthy Wood. That was our first meeting—there were others full of the pure enjoyment of just singing together and pooling our knowledge of old songs, and praising the music and poetry of some of her own folk musicians. Then one day the whole tribe went away on their travels, and I sat on the pony above on Birchanger Common and watched the caravans plodding along the Toll Road heading for Hookway and Oareford. The children were singing the inevitable 'Barbrew Ellen' as they went, and the wild air was one Dr. Joyce noted in 1847 in his *Ancient Music of Ireland*.

Among the treasures of song Cordelia left with me are three by her own people, which I feel should be set down for others. They show the grim humour, the careful turn of a good phrase and the single-minded faith of the best of the gipsies.

The first is 'The Broom Squire's Bird Song'. A Broom Squire

is a Quantock Hills gipsy and Cordelia described the composer to me. 'I did learn this from a Broom Squire near Over Stowey when I were knee high.' (He would probably be a Holland living there in the 1870's.) ' 'Twas all his own thought and the weaving of it. He were a true noble Christian old man.'

[TUNE TWENTY-FOUR]

THE BROOM SQUIRE'S BIRD SONG

Probably composed by old Duke Holland, Over Stowey, 1870, and sung by Cordelia Cooper at Worthy Wood above Porlock, 1943.

Of all the Birds that ever I see,
The Colley-bird[1] is the singer for me,
The Dove she croons for she would if she could,
The old cock Pheasant crows in the wood.
The Bullfinch pipes in the orchard tree,
But the Colley-bird is the singer for me.
The small Jenny Wren she has a loud song,
The Tits and the Sparrows they all go along.
The Hen she cackles again and again,
But the Colley-bird, the Colley-bird,
The Colley-bird carols after the rain.

The Curlew he cries far out on the hill,
The Rooks and the Jackdaws let go with a will,
The Nightingale sings in the still of the night,
The Thrush he hails the morning light,

[1] Colley-bird—blackbird.

64

The Linnet he goes it so sweet do he,
But the Colley-bird is the singer for me.
The Missel[1] he calls when the storm be strong,
The Ruddick[2] he cheers us when winter be long,
The Duck she quackles and quackles so plain,
But the Colley-bird, the Colley-bird,
The Colley-bird carols after the rain.

The Lark he sings praises high up in the air,
The little brown Dunnock[3] utters a prayer,
The Cuckoo calls Amen like a bell,
The swooping Swallow responds very well,
The Black-cap whistles so merrily,
But the Colley-bird is the singer for me.
And all the small birds the green bushes among
Sing Glory to God as I go along;
There's never a one that do praise in vain,
But the Colley-bird, the Colley-bird,
The Colley-bird carols after the rain.

The next is the grim humour of 'The Leaves They Do Fall'—a
shrewd comment on the danger and drama of a local problem
among scattered communities.

1 Missel—storm cock, missel thrush
2 Ruddick—robin.
3 Dunnock—hedge sparrow.

[TUNE TWENTY-FIVE]

THE LEAVES THEY DO FALL

Sung by Mrs. Cordelia Cooper, Hawkcombe Combe, Exmoor, 1943.

There was a rich farmer who died.
To all his sad children he cried,
'*There's gold for to spend,*
To be sharèd by all;
But when Death he do call,
As the leaves they do fall,
It will come to the last in the end, the end.'

Then his children they died, one by one,
And then said his dear youngest son,
'*There is gold for to spend*
To be sharèd by all,
But when Death he do call,
As the leaves they do fall,
It will come to the last in the end, the end.'

He was taken for murder was he,
There was twelve was to die on the tree,
He was last in the line,
To be sharèd by all,
But when Death he did call,
As the leaves they do fall,
It did come to the last in the end, the end.

The last is a gipsy carol by a member of her own tribe. 'To
show people that we are as good Christians as they.' I shall never
forget the magnificent voice of the tall, spare old woman as she

stood and sang it, altering time and melody as the mood took her, a memorable mixture of fire and mourning and a tenderness that whispered and faded into the silent watching woods.

[TUNE TWENTY-SIX]

THE WORTHY WOOD CAROL

Sung by Mrs. Cordelia Cooper above Ashley Coombe, August 1943. Composed by an Exmoor Gipsy, probably a Lock, in the 1920's or earlier.

Sleep my darling, darling little son,
Sleep my lovely, lovely little one,
For the world is heavy gold
For your little hands to hold.
Sleep then,
Sleep my darling, darling little son.

Sleep my darling, darling little son,
Sleep my lovely, lovely little one,
You've a-come to die for we
All upon the Criss Cross Tree,
Sleep then,
Sleep my darling, lovely little son.

Sleep my darling, darling little son,
Sleep my lovely, lovely little one,
For the Dear God he don't mind
If you finds us too unkind,
Sleep then,
Sleep my darling, lovely little son.

67

12

Mr. Barry, the Ballad Singer

Taunton and Kingston St. Mary, 1911

When he was tramping the Taunton Deane area he stayed in the Tramps' Lodging House down East Reach, and issued forth on his rounds each morning with half a dozen ballads in hand, and as many stuck in the band of his battered top-hat. He trudged miles, up farm lanes and into remote hamlets, and attended all local Markets and Fairs, but he was growing very old and his journeys were getting feebler and shorter. He still managed to bring back the pennies for his lodging and a couple for food, but with the winter coming again he was beginning to worry about his future.

He liked Taunton and would return there from Bristol, or Yeovil, or Dulverton at fairly regular intervals and, like Tommy Tucker, would 'sing for his supper' by a country lane-side as willingly as in a market.

I first saw and heard him in 1905 near Bishops Lydeard where he was standing and singing in the Gore, partly submerged in a passing herd of cows. I only heard a fragment of his ballad as we drove past but later found a copy, priced one penny, hand-printed on lavatory paper. There was an itinerant printer at the lodging house who turned out a few for him for the price of a supper, and this one was 'Old Harry and the Robber'.

[TUNE TWENTY-SEVEN]

OLD HARRY AND THE ROBBER

Sung by Mr. Barry, the Ballad singer and others, Taunton Deane, 1904–11.

Oh there were a robber, a right roaring heller,
And he did put fear, put fear in all.
The maids took and run when they heard him a-come,
And they heard how the robber did call:

'*Oh, I'm a fine feller, a right roaring heller,*
Now you're a-coming along with me!'

The ponies and the cows and the pigs in the sty,
The ducks and the geese and all, and all,
The sheep they did tremble when they did assemble,
And they heard the robber call.

He took from the rich and he took from the poor,
He did put fear, put fear in all,
When a rich man in black rode on to his track,
And they heard the robber call.

But the rider had horns hid under his hat,
Hoofs and horns and a tail and all,
The robber turned white at this horrible sight,
When he heard Old Harry did call:

'*Oh, I'm a fine feller, a right roaring heller,*
Now you're a-coming along with me!'

NOTE His Satanic Majesty like the elfin folk must never be called out-
right by his name. He is therefore politely referred to as 'Bogey', 'Old
Nick', 'The Gentleman Downstairs' and 'Old Harry'. 'Yew speak of the
Devil and he's standing right behind you,' i.e., you have called him up.

It was very popular round Norton Fitzwarren and Staplegrove I found, and then, like so many, became superseded with music-hall catchy airs which the old man left to younger, bawdier singers.

He never sang anything but old ballads or his own free verses on local happenings, and would, I was told, make 'up on the spot' songs about the Diamond Jubilee, and the Relief of Mafeking, or a burglary at a neighbouring manor—a Somerset singing commentator and purveyor of news many years before the West Indian Calypso became known all over the world.

I caught a rather distant glimpse of his top-hat and its ballads one crowded market day in Taunton when I was in adult company, so a closer look and listen was strictly taboo.

The true meeting came in the summer of 1911 (his very last) in a steep farm lane below Buncombe Hill. The farm girl and I were picking wild strawberries when he appeared on his upward climb, his boots slung round his neck. I admit I was scared at the top-hatted apparition seen close to. He was very tall, and hollow cheeked, with silver hair to his shoulders and he wore a frock coat, green with age but neatly tied together with bits of string, and a pair of much-patched corduroy trousers far too large for him, that the wife of some giant farmer had paid his singing with. He faltered to a stop—two young maids wouldn't have anything to give for his singing—but the farm was still up a steep rise and the chance of a bit of bread was dreadfully distant. Mary had a heart of gold, she was also bound for Kingston St. Mary with a whole penny of her wages to spend. 'You do look all tuckered out, Mr. Barry,' she said. 'Do 'ee rest a bit on this grass and have a strawberry or so. I've a penny for a ballad when you fetch your breath.' So we all sat on the bank among dusty laneside grasses under the hot sun and shared the strawberries, then I watched fascinated while he carefully and slowly put on his dilapidated boots, laced them neatly with string and stood up—he never sang barefoot and he always courteously raised his top-hat. He did so now to the two

70

little thirteen-year-old farm girls and said in the cultured accents of some Varsity don, 'My profound thanks to you young ladies. I will now endeavour to sing you the ballad of "The Murthered Son".' Endeavour was the correct description, for his voice was very weak and came gustily with obvious racking pauses for breath, but time did not matter to us and we were enthralled. I sat on the other side of Mary, for safety, for there was a queer shadow resting on his head and shoulders and I suddenly felt cold—but as I was recovering from a serious illness I didn't think much about it, the ballad absorbed my mind.

[TUNE TWENTY-EIGHT]

THE MURTHERED SON

Sung by Mr. Barry in a Buncombe Lane, August 1911.

A fine jolly soldier came a-riding along, along,
All on his way homewards a-singing this song:

My parents were honest but poor,
When I marched away to the War;
Now there's gold in my pocket of bounty a store,
And they'll never know want no more.

To his home then he came all a-riding along, along,
His parents they don't know him, a-singing this song.

'Come rest, my fine soldier, from a-riding along, along,
There's a fine feather bed just for singing this song.'

As he lay asleep after riding along, along,
They cutted his throat and they ended his song.

71

His horse they did sell for the riding along, along,
But a farmer came by and he heard the ghost song.

Oh what have you done to him riding along, along,
'Tis your own dearest son that was singing the song,

In old Tyburn cart you'll go riding along, along,
And all honest people will join in this song.

His parents were honest and poor
When he marched away to War.
At the hands of Jack Ketch, their necks will be stretched,
And they'll never know want no more.

About half-way through, Mary's kind, strong hand reached out
and pulled the shaky old man down beside us again, 'Yew can sing
the rest a-sitting comfortable for the once,' she told him. So he
did, and when he received her penny, again raised the top-hat. 'A
peaceful spot,' he said, looking at the sunny lane with its fox-

NOTE   This, of course, is a tale going back to very ancient times; this
version might be early eighteenth century or late seventeenth with its
naming of the hangman.

There is a West Country folk tale in which the soldier meets and
recognizes his brother, who, however, cannot return home with him.
When he does come back all ready for rejoicing the murder has been
committed.

Another Welsh Border tale gives the tragic recognition by his mother
of her son's deformed foot; and there are many more.

There must have been many such disappearances of travellers and
pedlars in remote times and areas.

I heard it sung by Trug Rich the harbourer on the Quantock Hills. He
had heard it at Bridgwater Fair in his youth about 1880.

gloves and drone of bees and cheerful yellow-hammer trills, 'but time presses for me, and Winter lies before me,' and he removed the boots and strung them about his neck, and stood up. He stalked away slowly and shakily round the next curve in the lane.

'Our varm ban't Winter's,' said Mary matter-of-factly. 'The poor old being be getting his wits all abroad. Missus will see to it he d'get his fill of broken meat and there's a old pair cowman's boots she've a-put by vor he. There be a wonderful plenty of strawberries hereabouts.' So we picked and ate and I no longer felt the cold. How could I in that Quantock lane under a hot summer sun? The next year when I met Mary she had news for me. 'Poor old Mr. Barry be gone! Died that very day you see him. A-coming down vrom Farm again he were and a-sat down the very spot we was to in the morning. A-putting on his new boots, Missus give 'en, sitting and lacing they up and he must have go'ed. They say 'twas his heart. Just up and died where you felt so cold.' I never told Mary about the chime child shadow I had seen, but I wondered if *he* knew and was putting on his new strong boots to sing courteously in the Heavenly Choir.

13

Isaiah Sully

Somerset folk singer and dancer,
born 1825, died 1923
Mainly West Somerset and Taunton Deane

Among the old folk singers I knew and visited whenever I could,
Isaiah Sully stands pre-eminent. He was easily the most outstand-
ing, he was also quite easily the most wicked.

He came, one gathered through comments dropped over the
twenty years I knew him, of a stock reaching back through the
centuries to the travelling minstrels who journeyed from castle to
castle and early manor in Somerset, singing and dancing and earning a full meal wherever they went. They most probably followed
their feudal lords through the French wars in the fourteenth
century, and, returning with them to a more peaceful England,
were given permission to travel whenever their Lords did not
require their immediate services. Many of the disjointed ancient
fragments of ballads I heard were suggestive of French Romaunts.
His name, too, was French, although as Taunton had received its
invasion of Huguenot refugees in the seventeenth century, it was
not therefore noticeable. Of course, his name was *not* Isaiah Sully.
(I have carefully selected a professional one for him, for some of
his second family may be still alive and might be very upset to
realize that for all their suppression of his public artistic works
he *was* more than a sinner plucked from the burning by their
united efforts.)

As a foot-loose young fellow in the 1840's, he was in demand
at every local fair in the South-Western Counties. As a singer he

was notable for the purity of his voice and *his subject matter!* His acting, however, was something else again, and the quick wit and scurrility of his dialogue was in direct folk play tradition. As a dancer he must have been agile indeed—some steps I saw him do as a child were an intricate and fine show of foot-work with some wonderful leaps. He would then have been round eighty.

One would have thought with all these gifts that his name would have become a legend in his life-time, but it was not so, and his second family's reticence is to be respected. To use the carefully non-commital West Somerest phrase—'he was not well-liked'. In other words, he was suspected, and quite rightly, of 'dark dealings'. Wherever throughout the years, and in whichever county or district he was a leading Mummer, Morrisman or Singer, his prowess was respectfully acknowledged. But the community heaved a sigh of relief when he travelled on as he so frequently did, and husbands no longer carried salt in their pockets, and wives and daughters no longer crossed feet or thumbs, or carried hidden a bit of a criss-cross in case they caught a glimpse of him.

For this reason I imagine very few of his gold-mine of songs were sung round farm firesides and at work as less worthy echoes of broad-sheets were. His shadow lay over the singer of them.

Now his first wife's songs were highly valued and popular—I often heard several which Mr. Cecil Sharp has collected in one region.

If she were anything like her only daughter, whom I met after her up-country marriage, she was a dear, dumpy, rosy soul with a completely matter-of-fact mind, and a voice like an autumn robin—clear, cold and sweet. The daughter had a very long memory for ballads (forty verses some of them!) and a wide repertoire, but was always on the listen to collect the old man's which he took malicious care she never did!

When her marriage took her far away the danger passed, for

his son Isaiah II had a beautiful voice, but a preference for the type of pot-house ditty as popular in Babylon as in this England of 1964. My own opinion was that this was purely a defence measure. He left home as a lad and went away to work on nearby farms, but he never married and though his memory was available for others for folk-play or dance, he would never perform. He was afraid to, having a firm belief in his father's 'dark powers.'

And so it came about that such of Isaiah Sully's treasured hoard as the bad old man decided to sing at all were sung to a child. A Chime Child, mind you, one of the 'gifted' by right of birth, who would appreciate the taboo matters unearthed and passed on, and who could not be affected by evil powers.

I happened to be that child.

I first met the old man as a bent, crippled figure tucked into a fireside chair, in the spotless cottage where he was living under the thumb of a highly respected second wife, who, the village said, collected and married him when he was in a drunken haze as the only way of saving a soul from Satan.

She must have been a courageous woman for she brought up his large family to be as grimly religious as herself, and applied their forty years of married life to saving Isaiah's soul. He was desperately afraid of her. Her steadfast uprightness was daunting although her kindness to me was very tender. After his marriage he was not allowed to sing, act or dance but must conduct himself as a 'saved soul'. In one thing only did he defy her, he never attended the meeting house of their very rigid sect (he dare not), neither did he attend any religious services elsewhere (again he dare not), and with that she had to be content.

Not so the family. Here was a lost sinner living in their very home and they laboured against a sense of guilt and failure throughout his life. This accounts for their many moves from their always exquisitely clean cottages to others which soon became as exquisitely clean and pervaded with their despairing sense of guilt.

Isaiah, of course, delighted in a grim silence punctuated by waspish comments on occasion. As a sheer mass they reduced him to a defensive taciturnity, but they never broke him, and after he was crippled in his sixties he seemed absolutely at their mercy— although the unsettling moves time after time could always be traced back to his own malicious public reminders of his old reputation.

Besides, they were never quite sure how crippled he really was. I wasn't either, but then I saw him in action when the family were away down the garden or in the hayfield, and his sudden flinging aside of his wraps and his agile capers round the kitchen table and back into his chair as a huddled mummy again, all in a moment, left me breathless with delight.

But of course I didn't mention them. I was a chime child, and the odd, and even uncanny, were my natural portion I found, whether I wished it or not, so my silence, like Isaiah's, was an habitual defence too.

If my own grown-ups were at the farm I have often been brought down to the cottage as a small girl and left to amuse 'Dad'.

'So crippley up as the poor, old dear be with they screws.'

I was regarded by house-bound womenfolk as a god-send whereby a half hour's free time down the garden could be snatched.

'The dear little soul, she do talk so clear and she do sing her little songs too. It do cheer 'en up.'

Yes, even poor Mrs. Second Isaiah turned a blind eye and a deaf ear on my small pipings. Whether she trusted in my manse upbringing and considered my repertoire consisted of Infant School Hymns, I shall never know, and somehow I never sang in front of her. But to Isaiah I blithely unburdened myself of nursery rhymes and singing games, ballads from Taunton market, and all the hotchpotch of music I hoarded, ranging from the Boer War 'Goodbye, Dolly, I must leave you' to the endless and horrifying murder of the eighteenth century, 'Cruel Ship's Carpenter'. And Isaiah replied in kind with a spate of song fragments, dance steps and even, on certain wonderful occasions, whole ballads one after another, impossible even for my very agile child memory to absorb except in large incomplete gollops.

He would never sing a song right through even in those childish days. He grew wilier still as I grew older, and his benevolence had a sudden uncertainty to it as unexpected as his lightning change from huddled cripple to Morrisman and back. In fact, only once did I really definitely learn anything of real worth from him. It proved very necessary later on.

Whether Isaiah himself foresaw this time and was, as he obviously believed, impelled to pass on a knowledge that would frustrate his own dark ways I don't know, but one afternoon he interrupted 'Barbarous Helen' to say sharply, 'Liddle Chime Child, ban't 'ee? Cassn't be overlooked or ill-wished not no-how. Gifted, ban't 'ee? Well, my maid, there'll come a time when 'ee'd best call this to mind.' And we spent a happy half hour singing this very old prayer of protection while Mrs. Second Isaiah picked currants for Taunton Market in blissful ignorance of the *singing* of *Popish* hymns in the third grim spotless cottage I had known.

[TUNE TWENTY-NINE]
PRAYER OF PROTECTION

Sung by Isaiah Sully, Taunton Deane, 1911.

First come Lord God,
And then come Holy Ghost,
And then come sweet Jesu, and then come sweet Jesu,
That died and loved us most.

Now blessèd be Lord God,
And blessèd Bright Trinity,
And bless us sweet Jesu, and bless us sweet Jesu
Who guard us wherever we be.

78

Glory to Lord God,
And Glory to Bright Trinity,
To Little Sweet Jesu that sleep under Star,
Singen all lustily.

There was a day many years and cottages later when I became
aware in the middle of singing 'Sweet Primeroses' that the ninety-
five-year-old helpless huddle of wraps, that Isaiah had by now
really become, was eyeing me with a piercing and deliberately
wicked gaze.

'Chime Child, ban't 'ee? Oh, ah! Cassn't be ill-wished,
hey?'

Whatever his malice was projecting from the depths of his
occult lore (or his insanity) it was overwhelming and terrifying,
and memory of the Prayer of Protection rose as a wall between us
and I sang it as if it were a continuation of the day's repertoire,
hoping I sounded as casual as I should like to have felt; and it
daunted him.

By the time I ended, he sat silent, his head on one side like a
magpie, and a magpie-like glint of wickedness fading from his eyes.
Then in an eager, oily voice he said, 'Now, I'll sing 'ee one,' and
gave me the entire song and ritual of 'The Standing Stones',
making sure I got it all down.

But that was Isaiah all through.

I left as soon as I decently could, still striving to be casual, but
on my way home I met Isaiah II, now over seventy, clumping

NOTE This is only to be sung when in some real danger as it is believed that any thoughtless singing of it is somehow interrupted or
spoiled like Isaiah's unfinished verses. It must never be used lightly

While describing this to interested friends on Christmas Eve 1964, I
was asked to sing it to them. I tried but found words and tune failed
with each effort, until I remembered and desisted.

wearily home to his lonely cottage. For once he stopped, looked at me with his faded blue eyes, so unlike his father's, and said slowly, 'Ah, I did a-wonder if the day 'ood come when he couldn't a-bear not to try out his powers. A chime child be a challenge, Miss Ruth, so you take and carry salt to your pocket.' And he slouched on in case too much had been said.

But the next time, months later, I went to see Isaiah I had remembered the hasty warning and am not ashamed to own now that I acted upon it.

We had a very pleasant but profitable short visit. Isaiah was looking tired and I was, to be quite frank, not too happy, so Mrs. Second Isaiah's free time was sadly curtailed, poor soul.

Two years passed and with them the memories of queer, quiet malice. I remembered only the hard work of years and the triumph of piecing this and that together—lovely single lines, a couplet with a dramatic beginning deliberately cut off, and something else less worth while repeated in its place because Isaiah saw my awakened interest and amused himself by frustrating it. One learned to wait for precious lines and even stanzas over years, solely by not showing any undue interest. The 'Gay Green Gown', for instance, took some fifteen years of fitting in a scattered mosaic of phrases and air—and there were others still fragmentary. I had hardly gained a footing into his vast store-house of song and dance in twenty years; there must be a hundred left. Was the old man still alive and, if so, what village had they moved to now?

I traced them to the newest cottage—Mrs. Second Isaiah had just died and the old sinner sat mute before a grand-daughter-in-law as large, solid and fanatical as the rest; waited until she left us for a precious ten minutes of freedom for her, and then announced gleefully, 'I told the old Missus I'd see her off to her Heavenly ways afore she drove I Downstairs. Oh ah, and I done it. 'Tis a true time for singing,' and with that he broke into a song I had long waited for, with a beautiful strange old air.

Alas! his married daughter, who had come on a visit of condolence, walked in upon us.

'Why, Dad, I never knowed you knowed that,' she exclaimed in triumph.

Isaiah stopped in mid phrase, 'Ah, my lass, if 'ee knowed all I know, you'd know a lot too much!' and he sank back with the magpie glint well lit up in the look of dislike her eavesdropping had earned.

Even her thick head perceived this at last, and she went off down the garden to discuss the funeral and its details with her in-law. 'Tryin' to poach what she've never no right to,' says Isaiah. 'My songs ban't for the like of she. Gifted folk be a different matter.' And though the moment was a bad one and I didn't expect much co-operation I said I should not see him again for some time (I never did), and had he passed on his store of folk music?

He sat in a grim huddle. His songs, despite his evil life, had been beautiful and cared for as rigidly as any ritual. Who was worthy of such a heritage?

Now one day, years back, I had gone along one of our deepsunk lanes, and heard a man working in an upland field above, singing as he worked. The voice was a fine one and I knew it, and the song was as lovely and fresh as the spring canopy of catkins and primrose banks that hid us from each other. For once Isaiah II had been carried past his lifelong fear by the joy of a Somerset Spring.

'Why don't you let young Isaiah learn a few for you?' I urged, knowing the response.

It was immediate.

'No! The bye idn' old enough.' (He must have been seventy-five.) 'Let he go down Pub and sing his songs there. Puppies do like muck!'

I never saw Isaiah again. He outlived Mrs. Second Isaiah by less than eight weeks.

Some of those days are fifty years away and his strange or lovely songs are hopelessly lost, but in the hope that there are many who treasure old lore and have long outgrown a puppy diet even today, I append two uncanny ballads of his—only to be sung at the 'proper time of year' and both concerning the magic and danger of green— the fairy colour worn by fairy ladies whose light morals were often a cloak for sinister death.

[TUNE THIRTY]

THE GAY GREEN GOWN

Collected from Isaiah Sully over a period of sixteen years, from 1904–20.

The Proud Ladye she rode through the wood,
And there in her way the Wicked One stood.
'Now welcome, Proud Ladye, Light down! Light down!
For I must give thee a gay green gown.
'Twill punish thy pride, for no honest Bride
Wears such a gown, wears such a gown—a gay green gown.'

The Proud Ladye rode out of the wood,
And her tears fell fast for her maidenhood.
'I will not cause my mother to frown,
I will not sully my Father's Crown—
With my little pen-knife I will take my young life.'
And all for a gown, all for a gowne—a gay green gown.

The Proud Ladye she laughed in scorn
'No Imp of the Pit by me shall be born!
Now God me forgive that I take my own life,
For maid am I none, and I'll never be wife.

A Leman of Hell,[1] in flames I must dwell
All for a gown, all for a gown—a gay green gown.'

The Proud Ladye she stabbed so deep
Her heart's blood trickled down to her knee.
The gown that was green was crimson to see
And red, red, red was her winding sheet.
Now let the bell toll for this Lost Ladye's soul
And all for a gown, all for a gown—a gay green gown.

[TUNE THIRTY-ONE]

THE GREEN LADY

*Verses 2 and 3 are compiled from lines and fragments of the much longer
ballad Isaiah sang in tantalizing occasional phrases during the period
1904 to about 1919.*

Now all you young fellows take heed what I tell.
Adown in the wood a Green Lady do dwell.
Her hair it is green and all green is her gown
And she calleth to all, 'Come here! Draw near!'
But she means them no good for she drinks their hearts' blood;
They never do wed, for they takes to their bed,
And they dies—they all dies at the end of the year.
All under the tree
There sits a Green Lady.

NOTE In this mixture of very early and medieval church beliefs the
punishment of breaking a taboo entails eternal degradation. There was a
Lost Lady Wood in mid-Somerset, since cut down.

[1] Leman of Hell—the Devil's mistress.

Now all you young fellows take heed what I tell:
Adown in the wood a Green Lady do dwell.
And a bush lad drew nigh with a roving eye
And she called to him, 'Draw near! Come here!'
But his sweetheart she ran and caught hold of her man
And she took him away and to him did say
'You shan't die. You shan't die at the end of the year.'
All under the tree
There sits the Green Lady.

Now all you young fellows take heed what I tell.
Adown in the wood a Green Lady do dwell.
To the wood then she goes in his breeches and hose
And the Green Lady called, 'Draw near! Come here!'
But a little axe had she, hid down by her knee,
And she chopped down the tree and the Green Lady
And they died—yes they died—at the end of the year.
All under the tree
There sits a Green Lady.

NOTE   A chilling but fairly complete picture of a dangerous nature spirit, of the vampire type. Any wood called Green Ladies was sedulously avoided—not only for the fairy claim upon it but in case it harboured such a tree spirit. She is true sister to the East Anglian ghost quoted to me in 1956, by a schoolgirl:

> 'So they looked thro' the keyhole
> To see what they could see
> And there they saw The Green Lady
> *Dancing with the Devil in a Bowl of Blood!*'

There are only two folk tales about her in Folk Lore's early volumes, but in each the hint of a tree spirit is present.

The Music

of the Songs

THE BOLD PIGLET

There were a lid-dle pig - let, he wad-n't ve-ry old: ___ He runned a-way from whoame he did, he were so ve-ry bold.

NOTE The A flat is optional.

THE SHEPHERD AND HIS DOG

They be climb-ing up the hill, All our sheep, all our sheep; For the morn-ing air be chill, And the fields they lie still, And the wor-dle be a-sleep, ___ Say the Shep-herd and his dog. ___

85

TENDING THE SHEEP

Ex. 3

If I were the King of Ta'n-ton town, I'd wear a
sword and a gold-en crown; I'd ride on a-fore when we
went to the war,_ With sol-diers to foll-ow, a hun-dred or more.
But I'd rath-er be tend-ing my sheep, Yes I'd
rath-er be tend-ing my sheep; My ewes and my rams and my
lit-tle young lambs, I'd rath-er be tend-ing my sheep._____

BABEL TOWER

Ex. 4

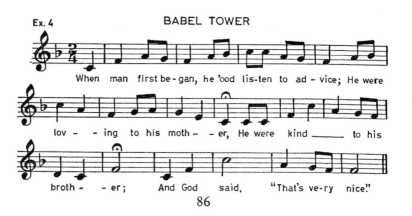

When man first be-gan, he 'ood lis-ten to ad-vice; He were
lov - - ing to his moth - - er, He were kind _____ to his
broth - - er; And God said, "That's ve-ry nice."

THE CAROL OF CHRIST'S DONKEY

Ex. 5

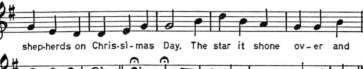

I gave Him my man-ger all full of sweet hay; I knelt with the

shep-herds on Chris-si-mas Day. The star it shone ov-er and

loud did I bray. Glor-i-a in ex-cel-sis! Christ the Lord is born!

GILLAVOR

Ex. 6

Gill-a-vor, Gill-a-vor, white and ro-sy red, Tell me tru-ly

if I shall wed. Shall I be a wid-ow, a moth-er or a wife, Or

shall I live sin-gle all my life? Tell me, What shall it be, A

wid-ow, wife or sin-gle all my life? For he loves me, he don't, He'll

have me, he won't, He would if he could but he can't.

87

THE POSY RHYME

The dai-sy, the dai-sy, she sits on the grass, Where lit-tle birds nest and the lit-tle lambs pass. She grows, oh she grows, in a fine sil-ver ring, And when there are twelve it is the_ sweet spring.

THERE GOES OLD TOM

There was an old Po-ny just twelve hands high (Hard a-way, hark away, there goes Old Tom.) His muz-zle was meal-y with a nice_ toad-eye. (Chorus:) Ov-er, Hup ov-er! (Echo:) Ov-er, hup ov-er! He'd hunt all out ov-er but nev-er in vain. (Hard a-way, hark a-way, there goes Old Tom.) And bring Farm-er home in the fog and the rain. (Ov-er, out ov-er! (Echo:) Ov-er, out ov-er!) At wall or wat-er when hounds did run on,

88

Ov - er or un - der or through went Old Tom,

(Ov - er, hup ov - er!) Hard a-way, hark a-way, there goes Old Tom.

OLD MOTHER EVE

Ex. 9

The ap-ple tree stood in the gar-den It's blossoms as white as the

snow,— the snow, And there in the cool of the eve-ning, Our dear Lord God He did

Quicker

go, He did go. But old Moth-er Eve she liked ap - ples, And

Ad-am he liked 'en too,— he liked 'en too,— he liked 'en too.

THE BRIAR AND THE OAKEN TREE

Ex. 10

Oh If I were a red, red bri - ar, and

you were an oak - en tree, I'd twine all a -bout and

bloss-om for thee. You'd hold me so closely my one on-ly

dear, And we'd live and we'd love for a hund - red year.

89

THE LILY SHE GROWS IN THE GREENWOOD

Ex. 11

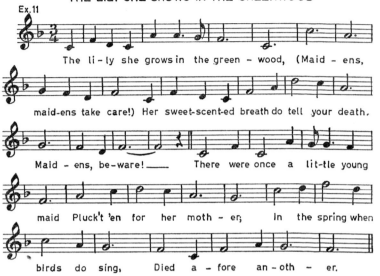

The li-ly she grows in the green - wood, (Maid - ens,

maid-ens take care!) Her sweet-scent-ed breath do tell your death,

Maid - ens, be-ware!____ There were once a lit-tle young

maid Pluck't 'en for her moth - er; In the spring when

birds do sing, Died a - fore an-oth - er.

THE GOOSE-FEATHER BED

Ex. 12

Young Jen - ny she sat all a - weep - ing, For

both her dear pa-rents were dead. The lar-der was bare, and no

mon-ey was there, All she had was a goose-feather bed.

Variation (1st half)

etc.

90

I TOOK MY DAME TO LAMBING FEAST

Ex. 13

I took my Dame to lamb-ing feast, We all sat down to sup-per. The ta-ble tipped and down she slipped, A-roll-ing in the but-ter. But up she got and ate the lot While we were all a-flut-ter. She gol-loped a bar-rel of ci-der brew So I cart-ed her home on a shut-ter.

THE SPUNKY

Ex. 14

The Spunk-y he went like a sad lit-tle flame, All, all a-lone,— All out on the zogs and a-down the lane, All, all a-lone.— A tin-ker came by that was full of ale, And in-to the mud he went head ov-er tail. All, all a-lone.

91

COLD LIES THE DEW

Ex. 15

There was an old Gran-ny who lost her sight (Cold lies the dew.__)She

couldn't tell if it were morn-ing or night, (Cold lies the dew.__) There

come a fine gen-tle-man black as a coal, "I'll give 'ee some eyes if you'll

sell me your soul," (Cold lies the dew.__) Sing-ing Green, green,

green,__ all a-green, all a-green,__ a-danc-ing round the tree.__

ON SEDGEMOOR
(The Marsh Fever)

Ex. 16

When the mist be all a-bout, Then let no man

ven - ture out. It will grip you, hale or stout, With - out

doubt. For Death he is a - walk - ing, a - walk - ing, a -

walk - ing, For to find his dead, And the mar - ish ground do

shiv - er to his tread. Lie _____ safe a - bed.

LANGPORT TOWN

By the beds of green withies a young man I es-pied, La-ment-ing his true love, la-ment-ing his bride. All on a sum-mer morn-ing she went to Lang-port town, But she nev-er comed home a-gain, she nev-er comed home a-gain, She nev-er comed home a-gain, when the moon it went down. Oh Ell-um do grieve, and Oak he do hate, But Will-ow, Will-ow, Will - - ow, Will-ow, Will-ow do walk if you trav el late.

MARY MAGDALENE

Ma - ry, Ma - ry, Ma - ry Mag-da-le - ne, She was a whore of Je - ru - sa - lem. She wore a green_ gown, when she laid her a-down, On a bed of pease_ straw._

NOTE 'Lass' may be sung instead of 'whore'.

THE TWELVE APOSTLES

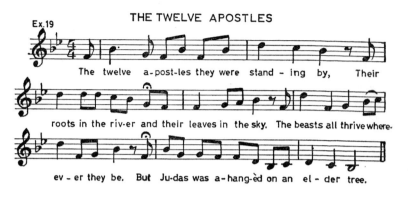

The twelve a-post-les they were stand - ing by, Their roots in the riv-er and their leaves in the sky. The beasts all thrive where-ev - er they be. But Ju-das was a-hang-èd on an el - der tree.

NUTTING ON SUNDAY

Oh there was a maid, and a fool-ish young maid, And she went a-nut-ting on Sun-day. She met with a Gen-tle-man all in black; He took and he laid her a - down on her back, All a - cause she went nut-ting on Sun - day.

NOTE An alternative may be sung—'She couldn't move for'ard, She couldn't move back.'

THE THREE DANISH GALLEYS

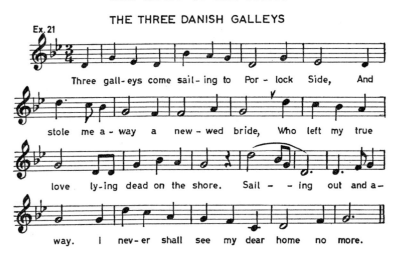

Three gall-eys come sail-ing to Por-lock Side, And stole me a-way a new-wed bride, Who left my true love ly-ing dead on the shore. Sail — — ing out and a-way. I nev-er shall see my dear home no more.

THE LAZY WAVE

The la — — zy wave slides ov-er the sand; My love and I were hand in hand. It ran till it came where we — did stand, And fad-ed a-way in the Sev-ern sand. Oh love that be new runs in on the tide, But love that be eb-bing will nev-er a-bide. Like the la — zy wave it do fade — a-way, And leave you a-lone for ev-er a day.

95

THE BREAN LAMENT

Ex. 23

The wat-ers they washed 'en a - shore, a - shore, And they
nev-er will sail — the seas — no more. We laid 'en a-
long by the church - yard wall, And all in a
row — we bu - ried them all. But their boots we
bu - ried be - low — the tide On Sev - ern side.

Variant

The gulls they fly ov - er so high, so — high, To
see where their bod-ies all safe do lie (They fly all around
and loud they do call)

THE BROOMSQUIRE'S BIRD SONG

Ex. 24

Of all — the birds that ev-er I see, The Coll - ey
bird is the sing - er for me. The Dove she croons for she
would if she could. The old cock Pheas-ant crows in the

wood. The Bull - finch pipes— in the or - chard tree,

But the Coll - ey bird is the sing - er for me. The

small Jen - ny Wren she has a loud song, The Tits and the

Spar-rows they all go a - long. The Hen she cackles a -

gain and a - gain, But the Coll- ey bird, the

Coll- ey bird, The Coll - ey bird car-ols af - ter the rain.

THE LEAVES THEY DO FALL

Ex. 25

There was a rich farm - er who died.——— To

all his sad child - ren he cried,——— "There's gold for to

spend, to be shar- èd by all; But when Death he do call, As the

leaves they do fall, It will come to the last in the end, the end."

THE WORTHY WOOD CAROL

Ex. 26

Sleep, my dar-ling, dar-ling lit-tle son, Sleep, my love-ly, love-ly lit-tle one. For the world is heav-y gold For your lit-tle hands to hold. Sleep __ then, Sleep, my dar-ling, love-ly lit-tle son.

OLD HARRY AND THE ROBBER

Ex. 27

Oh there were a rob-ber, a right roar-ing hell-er, And he did put fear, put fear in all. The maids took and run when they heard him a-come, And they heard how the rob-ber did call: "Oh I'm a fine fell-er, a right roar-ing hell-er; Now you're a com-ing a-long with me"

THE MURTHERED SON

Ex. 28

A fine jol-ly sol-dier came a-rid-ing a-long, a-long, All on his way home-wards a-sing-ing this song: "My par-ents were hon-est but poor _____ When I marched a-

98

way to the war____ Now there's gold in my pock-et of

boun-ty a store, And they'll nev-er know want no more."____

THE PRAYER OF PROTECTION

Ex. 29

First come Lord God, And then come Ho - ly

Ghost __ And then come sweet Je - su, and then come sweet

Je - su, That di - èd and lov - èd us most.____

THE GAY GREEN GOWN

Ex. 30

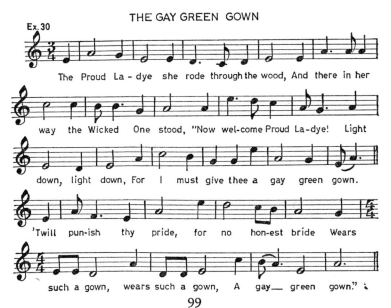

The Proud La - dye she rode through the wood, And there in her

way the Wicked One stood, "Now wel-come Proud La-dye! Light

down, light down, For I must give thee a gay green gown.

'Twill pun-ish thy pride, for no hon-est bride Wears

such a gown, wears such a gown, A gay__ green gown."

THE GREEN LADY

Ex. 31

Now all you young fellows take heed what I tell. A-down in the
wood a Green La-dy do dwell. Her hair__ it is green and all
green is her gown, And she call-eth to all, "Come here! Draw near!" But she
means them no good, for she drinks their heart's blood; They nev-er do
wed for they take to their bed,__ For 'tis Death,__cold Death do draw
near__ And they dies,__ they all dies__ at the end of the
year. All un-der the tree There sits a Green La-dye.

Index of Names
and Song Titles

'Annie's Granny', 35–41

Babel Tower, 11, 86
Barry, Mr., 68–73
Blackmore, Aunt Loveday, 30–33
Bold Piglet, The, 6–7, 85
Bond, Aunt Thurza, 28–29
Brean Lament, The, 60, 96
Briar and the Oaken Tree, The, 29, 89
Broom Squire's Bird Song, The, 64–65, 96–97

Carol of Christ's Donkey, 16–17, 87
Chime Children, 1–4
Cold lies the Dew, 42–43, 92
Cooper, Cordelia, 62–67
Criddle, Granny, 28–29, 31

Flynn, Delia and Patrick, 13–16, 18–21

Garland, Richard, 45–49
Gay Green Gown, The, 82–83, 99
Gillavor, 19
Gillavor White and Rosy Red, 20, 87
Goose-feather Bed, The, 32–33, 90
Green Lady, The, 83–84, 100

Hagarty, Alice, 13–16

I took my Dame to Lambing Feast, vii, 33, 91

Langport Town (The Water Witch), 48–49, 93
Lazy Wave, 59, 95
Leaves they do fall, The, 66, 97
Lewis, Mrs., 28
Lily she grows in the Greenwood, The, 30–31, 90

Mary Magdalene, 51–52, 93
Murthered Son, The, 71–72, 98–99

Nutting on Sunday, 54–55, 94

Odcombe, Delilah, 50–54
Old Harry and the Robber, 69, 98
Old Mother Eve, 26–27, 89
'Old Shepherd', 5–11, 29, 34
On Sedgemoor (The Marsh Fever), 47, 92

Posy Rhyme, 22, 88
Prayer of Protection, 78–79, 99

Shepherd and his Dog, The, 8–9, 85
Spunky, The, 41–42, 91

Strong, Mrs., 28
Sully, Isaiah, 47, 74–82

Tending the Sheep, 10, 86
There goes Old Tom, 24–25, 88–89

Three Danish Galleys, 57–58, 95
Twelve Apostles, 53, 94

Webber, William, 23
Winter, William, 34
Worthy Wood Carol, The, 67, 98